THE RETIREMENT RESIDENCE

THE
RETIREMENT
RESIDENCE

An Analysis of the Architecture and
Management of Life-Care Housing

By

JAMES FRUSH, JR.
Vice President, Retirement Residence, Incorporated
San Francisco, California

and

BENSON ESCHENBACH, A.I.A.
San Francisco, California

CHARLES C THOMAS · PUBLISHER
Springfield · Illinois · U.S.A.

Published and Distributed Throughout the World by
CHARLES C THOMAS · PUBLISHER
BANNERSTONE HOUSE
301-327 East Lawrence Avenue, Springfield, Illinois, U.S.A.
NATCHEZ PLANTATION HOUSE
735 North Atlantic Boulevard, Fort Lauderdale, Florida, U.S.A.

With THOMAS BOOKS *careful attention is given to all details of
manufacturing and design. It is the Publisher's desire to present books
that are satisfactory as to their physical qualities and artistic possibilities
and appropriate for their particular use.* THOMAS BOOKS *will be true
to those laws of quality that assure a good name and good will.*

Printed in the United States of America
H-2

PREFACE

There is a rapidly increasing fund of reference material accumulating on the problems of the elderly citizen. Until recently this was an almost unknown and unexplored field, but in the past five years a surprisingly prolific sequence of lectures, papers, articles, statistics, and books has been published which document and define the range of geriatrics and gerontology. Reference materials on homes for the aged, guardianship and protective services, centers for older people, medical care and health insurance, aging, religion and the church, preparing for retirement, a psychiatric approach to institutional work with the aged, and so forth illustrate the variety. However, despite this amazing and diverse publication, almost nothing has been presented for information and review on what may have a more critical impact on more aging persons than any other factor—namely, the economic criteria of the design and management of housing for our elders.

Unless income and expense statements are reasonably exact and provide an actual and realistic margin of reserve, we may be faced with an accounting scandal which will seriously affect the construction and operation of all retirement homes, but more tragically, which may affect hundreds of individuals, now residing in those homes, whose incomes, sufficient for the monthly fee quoted in the three-color advertising blurbs, may be inadequate to meet the actual increased costs encountered after the project has commenced operation.

Many projects have gone into default in the past few years. In nearly all instances the error is not one of malicious intent. The error, perhaps even more tragically since it involves people of goodwill, is compounded by ignorance—and not ignorance of a general nature, for the sponsorship of most organizations is composed of intelligent, often gifted leaders of a community—rather, ignorance of a highly specialized field which concerns the annual operating statement of an elderly housing project.

As an illustration—under the heading "Laundry and Cleaning":

[v]

How often should rooms be cleaned? How often should linen be changed? How will the expected occupancy of the infirmary affect the overall cost of laundry? Should all or part of the laundry be contracted? If in a particular area over 35 per cent of the laundry cost includes food service items, would it be more economical to launder these items on the premises, or would the economies be offset by increased labor costs? The detailed examination of costs described in this work may be illustrated by the complexity of the following operating criteria: food costs and services; resident transportation and trucking; infirmary supplies; furniture, equipment, and mechanical services; insurance—hospitalization, fire, automotive, liability, surgical, fidelity, malpractice, property damage, and so forth; replacement reserves; linen replacement; nursing payroll; patrol service; repairs; telephone; utilities—heat, light, elevator power, hot water, kitchen fuel, water, gas, and sewer. This list is partial and is further broken down under individual headings: for example, "Replacement Reserves" is comprised of those items whose life is of shorter duration than the mortgage, that is, which must be replaced before the mortgage is amortized. Items such as motors, paint, boilers, fixtures, kitchen equipment, roofing, and so forth all have various periods of obsolescence or wear, and these factors must be known and computed. The listing of some of the items in this complete range (only suggested by the short extract above) indicates the enormous amount of research and experience involved in operating criteria.

From the foregoing, it is apparent that inexperience or errors of omission or judgment can result, and unfortunately, have resulted in inaccuracies and underestimates so critical that they will jeopardize, by association, even the well-considered retirement project.

It is our hope that this text will illuminate and strengthen the analysis so necessary to assure the success of one of the most revolutionary ideas of our generation—the design, construction, and operation of a complete housing environment for the elderly.

JAMES FRUSH, JR.
BENSON ESCHENBACH

CONTENTS

THE
RETIREMENT
RESIDENCE

Section One

Chapter I

A NEW PROBLEM IN HOUSING
FOR OUR ELDERS

ONE OF THE recent changes in the composition of our society is the appearance of a numerically significant elderly population. To-day there are over twenty-five millions of Americans who are past sixty years of age; by 1970 this figure will climb to twenty-eight millions. It is interesting to note that this is greater than the population of the United States in 1850.

The increased number of persons living longer is strikingly demonstrated by the statistic that one out of every three persons sixty years of age or older has a living parent. Today it is common for persons to expect to have a life span which will extend into that equivocal classification referred to as the senior years.

Several reasons are given for this recent phenomenon. Some of these are advances in techniques of public health, increased knowledge in the field of medical science, and the defeat of fatal childhood diseases. Soon, further discoveries in the nature and treatment of the diseases of old age will add to man's already increased life span. At a time contemporaneous with the earliest settlement of the United States, Descartes put such trust in the rewards of science that he thought man some day may be able to treat "even the infirmities of age."

We must remember, however, that the United States is a young country. Our emphasis has been on youth. Sociologists sometimes refer to our culture as child-centered. Until recently, our national concern for the elderly has been limited to the indigent aged whose housing needs were solved by the old-age institution—an institution which relieved the conscience while keeping the old folks out of sight—an institution which by its nature exchanged hope for security. It was a life aptly described by Dr. Johnson as "rowing without a port."

In essence, the problem until recently has been an economic problem and partially a social problem. Today it is not only both economic and social, but because of the increased elderly population, arithmetical. It is necessary to find solutions for all economic and social strata of our elderly citizens.

In addition to medical, social and economic needs, the elderly person is confronted with a housing problem which is new and complex. While living alone is often an experience of loneliness and inadequacy, living with younger relatives has its obvious drawbacks. The suburban tract-house and the city apartment are, for the most part, incapable of housing a three-generation family even in moderate comfort.

Perhaps the most incredible aspect of our concern for the elderly as a social group is the rapidity with which the problem has arisen. Until a few years ago it was a problem which was left to religious and fraternal organizations; today it is almost regarded as a national crisis.

Chapter II

SOME INTERPRETATIONS OF HOUSING FOR OUR ELDERS

Many TYPES OF HOUSING are necessary. This book deals primarily with life care, the most complex interpretation of housing needs. It is necessary, however, to dwell momentarily on other types of housing. Aside from being of general interest, it will help delineate life care by describing housing solutions which are sometimes confused with life-care housing but in fact are not.

PUBLIC HOUSING

Public housing is rental housing which is publicly owned and operated. Its purpose is to provide basic housing for persons whose income is below a locally established level. While it is not necessarily intended (except incidentally) for elderly persons, many elderly persons live in public housing developments because of financial necessity.

Its purpose, again, is basic housing and only basic housing. There are, however, experiments which indicate new trends. A development in South Dakota which provides communal dining is an example; the dining room is operated by a local agency. Another example is in Pittsburgh where a community organization provides house-cleaning services. A common variation is to include recreational and counselling services.

There is no doubt that public housing solves an excruciating need. Nonetheless, it (like most housing for our elders) is limited to elderly persons who are ambulatory and can live independently (in the complete sense of the phrase). Any health facilities must be community-operated. This is excellent as long as a person is physically and mentally able to maintain his or her household. The inability, however, of most persons to continue indefinitely without services, soon becomes apparent to anyone working in the field of gerontology.

If an elderly resident becomes debilitated or incapacitated in any manner whatsoever, his housing predicament is worsened. The experiments mentioned above are an effort to meet this obvious social defect within a workable economic framework.

LOW-RENTAL HOUSING

Under Section 202 of the National Housing Act, Government funds have been made available for low-rental housing by direct loans at a low interest rate. Its purpose is to provide housing for elderly persons of the low-middle income bracket—in other words, persons whose income is too high for public housing and inadequate for commercial apartments or dwellings. Here, too, the trend is toward incorporating certain communal facilities into the operation of the project. These are generally in the form of dining and recreational facilities.

APARTMENT AND MEALS

Many nonprofit organizations have recognized the need of what social agencies refer to as boarding homes and have provided facilities which are exemplary from an ethical and moral standpoint. Generally, medical needs cannot be fulfilled on the premises since such services require expenditures beyond the capacity of the home. The exception is when medical care is given by a religious order whose members devote their lives to caring for the aged. Housing of this type has been realized in some instances through Section 231 of the National Housing Act. Generally it serves the food and housing needs of the middle and upper-middle income level.

RESIDENTIAL HOTELS

Many residential hotels provide excellent temporary housing. While a person is fully ambulatory his needs are met. Usually such hotels are located downtown, which may or may not be an advantage.

Unfortunately, certain proprietors lacking in a social sense have found the elderly to be a captive market. Consequently, hotels of the skid-row variety have been reconverted to "hotels for senior citizens." While some hotels, through rehabilitation, may be suitable, many are beyond any but superficial improvements. Tragically, the prognosis points to the tenements of ten years hence.

RETIREMENT COMMUNITIES

Throughout the United States, dozens of tracts with recreational centers have been constructed to fulfill the retirement needs of the middle-aged and young elderly. They offer cheap housing and ownership. They are usually self-contained little communities located far from urban centers, where land is cheap. Some are excellent; others are quite unsatisfactory.

At least one developer, however, has recognized the need for extensive medical care and has incorporated an admirable medical program into his communities. Otherwise—save recreational facilities and grab-bars—they are almost identical to any other medium-cost housing tract. Any conjecture as to the eventual fate of such communities, when the now-active population becomes truly elderly, is horrendous.

A one- or two-paragraph description of important housing solutions is inadequate. Nonetheless, it is sufficient to realize that each has its advantages and disadvantages. Each exemplifies a genuine housing need.

LIFE CARE

Now let us take a closer look at the requirements of our elders. According to the findings of the Scottish Housing Authority in a study of the ambulatory aged:
a. Fifteen per cent cannot clean house.
b. Twelve per cent cannot prepare meals.
c. Twenty-seven per cent cannot wash clothes.
d. Sixteen per cent cannot shop.
Again—according to a paper recently delivered at the National Conference on the Aging—of the "older persons in our country not living in chronic hospitals or nursing homes":
a. Twenty-six per cent have one chronic medical condition.
b. Twenty per cent have two chronic medical conditions.
c. Thirty-one per cent have three or more chronic medical conditions.

　　d. Twelve per cent have a chronic limitation of mobility.

　　e. Thirty-one per cent have a chronic limitation of activity.

These are but two of hundreds of such examples which may be found in any gerontological or public health library. They are sufficient, however, to bring the purpose of life care into focus.

It has been apparent for many years that housing in itself will not fulfill the requirements of elderly persons. An all-encompassing phrase —life care—was used to describe housing which included such services as meals, medical care, maid and room-cleaning services, recreational activities, and so on. Presently the expression life care came to have a legal as well as descriptive significance. In the State of California, for instance, any organization or person who receives property from an aged person conditioned upon an agreement to furnish life care or care for a period of more than one year is subject to the laws relating to life care. Obviously, care for one year and a day is usually not care for life.

When we speak of life care throughout this book, we are referring to care for life in both the legal and descriptive sense of the word. A first-rate life-care retirement residence, for example, will provide the following:

　　a. Apartment accommodations.

　　b. Three meals each day.

　　c. Nearly total medical and hospital care without deductions or time limitations.

　　d. Room-cleaning service.

　　e. Personal service (help with dressing, bathing, and so forth when needed).

　　f. Utilities.

　　g. Recreational program.

Most important, all of this is still provided if for some reason a resident becomes financially debilitated. Life care, in other words, includes housing as an important provision but not as *the* most important provision. The extent of services is such that life care is not only different in degree from other examples of housing for our elders: it it different in type.

Chapter III

THE ARCHITECTURAL PROGRAM
DESCRIPTION

AN ARCHITECTURAL PROGRAM is a statement of requirements. It can be as simple as the fundamentals of basic shelter or as involved as a metropolitan complex. Usually the client who retains an architect has a reasonably exact knowledge of his requirements or program. He states this program to his architect as succinctly and directly as he is able, and his architect in turn translates these thoughts into ideas, sketches, and finally into structure. A client who plans to build a house, for example, speaks of his family—their personalities, ages, likes, and dislikes. He tells of his budget and finances. He describes the area or location which he prefers. He talks of rooms (number and size), their use and relation, and notes furniture and furnishings he prefers. As these conferences are continued and the rapport developed between client and architect, the program and requirements are further refined until the closest approach to their ideal is gained.

In varying degrees, but with increasing involvement, this procedure is followed in large, more complicated projects. Whether the client is a family planning a home, a school board scheduling a school, a board of directors projecting an office building, or a vestry planning a church, the method of programming is the same; that is, the client who intimately realizes his present and future requirements relates them to his architect for translation into space and structure.

When we enter the particular field with which we are concerned, life-care housing for our elders, we meet an anomalous problem. The client (usually a nonprofit organization) is not only unfamiliar with architectural and structural needs but is likewise unversed in related economics, financing, and management. The one invaluable quality these sponsors demonstrate, without which no program is successful, is the warm, humanitarian recognition of this problem that must be resolved—the understanding, care, and consideration of their elders.

[11]

This lack of program knowledge places an uncommonly heavy burden upon the architect. He must assume and state the program, create plans of resolution, and finally check the plans for conformance to program. We have had the fortune to study in detail all of the major retirement projects in the West—an area which has pioneered this field. We have had the further fortune to test the conclusions these studies have developed with our own designs of life-care projects—from simple residential-type suburban plans like Canterbury Woods in Pacific Grove, California, to high-rise metropolitan centers like The Tamalpais in Larkspur, California. From this study, in theory and in practice, were generated the ideas and ideals which we will describe, with the hope that they may lighten the task of others.

REQUIREMENTS

The order of description of a program is at best haphazard. In our description of our theoretical family-home program, we described first the family itself, then budget and income, then location, then room areas, and finally, furnishings. This order of listing could be reversed or interchanged. The only important requirement is that the list be complete. Perhaps the most direct way to write the program would be to list first the known facts then follow with the estimated requirements.

Apartments

Family Size

The average age of those who enter a life-care retirement residence is 74.5 years. The average age of all residents after a project has been in operation for about fifteen years levels out at about 82.6.

There are at entrance between seventy and eighty single persons out of every one hundred. This means that about 83 per cent of apartments are occupied by single persons. It should be recognized, however, that single-occupancy apartments are not all studios. Many are alcove or one-bedroom and, on rare occasion, a single person who enjoys receiving guests will reserve a two-bedroom apartment.

After the residence has been in operation for about fifteen years, the proportion of single persons to couples gradually increases to

95 per cent. This change, frequently representing lowered income for the surviving single person, also means a marked change in apartment demand; the trend of course is to smaller, less-expensive apartments. The flexibility needed to accommodate this change must be designed into the original structure. Unless this basic change in resident-population characteristic is anticipated in the original planning, then unnecessarily expensive changes or excessive vacancies with resultant economic impact must later occur.

Types of Apartments

The proportioning of apartment sizes, that is, the relative per cent of studio, alcove, one- and two-bedroom apartments, is related of course to the economics of the project—whether located in or directed toward a middle-income group, upper-middle income group, or wealthy class. Obviously, both space and apartment room-count are related to income, although studies indicate that in our increasingly "affluent society" the variation is not as great as might be expected. As examples, from two representative groups we have experienced these demands:

	Studio	Alcove	1-Bdrm	2-Bdrm
Middle income	55%	25%	15%	5%
Upper income	35%	18%	32%	15%

Before detailing the varied apartment arrangements, let us first list the common qualities: Each apartment has a small kitchenette. This seems, perhaps, an unwarranted expense since three daily meals are served in the main dining room, but we have learned that while the average woman may be ready to end a lifetime of meal scheduling and cooking, she nevertheless does not want to be denied the pleasure of serving friends in her own apartment; or preparing those special cookies which are a Christmas tradition, or that recipe which has long been a family favorite; or perhaps relaxing with a Sunday brunch in the privacy of her own apartment. Cooking has usually been a lifetime vocation and, as she may say, "I like to keep my 'hand in.' "

Each apartment has its own secluded balcony, large enough for easy chairs and a small table. A balcony serves three useful purposes: (1) the sliding doors opening onto the terrace greatly extend the sense of space, especially when compared to the usual small apartment window; (2) the terrace or balcony provides a delightful area for sunning, dining, or just plain relaxing; and (3) summertime use in the East, all-year in the West, permits a small flower- or plant-garden which adds an interesting personal note to the setting.

Each apartment has an entrance foyer and closet to provide a pleasant transitional area between the public spaces and the apartment. Each apartment provides exceptional closet space. Almost invariably, those who join a retirement center move from a larger home, and even with generous storage-space, the task of limiting treasured possessions is difficult. In addition to the storage space within the apartment, an absolute minimum space of 3 by 4 by 6 ft should be provided in the basement for trunks, suitcases, boxes and so on.

Each apartment has a lever switch-plate noted "Emergency Call" which enables the resident to summon help immediately, if needed. These switches are located in easily accessible places in every room. Each apartment (and public space) has a fire-sensing device, either a smoke detector or a heat-actuated sprinkler, which sounds an alarm in the central control where someone is on duty day and night, and simultaneously registers in the nearest fire-station.

Each apartment has a well-located television outlet connected to a single main-antenna tower. Each apartment has a telephone from which local calls may be dialed and which is switchboard-connected (as in a major hotel) to provide services when requested.

The varied apartment arrangements consist of four basic types: The smallest is the studio, a living-bedroom-combination main room. Next is the alcove type, a living room with bed alcove opening into the living room, but with a *shoji* or folding screen which can be drawn to divide the alcove from the living room. The next larger unit is the one-bedroom type, a standard arrangement with separate living and bed rooms. Largest is the two-bedroom apartment, also standard with a private bath with each bedroom. As mentioned earlier, although it is usual that the residents bring with them the furniture which they prefer, carpets and draperies are always provided by management. Often the pieces of furniture may appear inappropriate or out of scale to the apartment, but moving from a long-loved home into a new setting is at best a trying experience and, as one minister said in metaphor, "When we transplant flowers it is always wise to move along as much native soil as we can."

A planning concept which we have endeavored to use in our projects is the extensive employment of corner apartments. In any project, from small residence to towering office-building, corner locations are most desirable for three fundamental reasons:

a. They provide cross ventilation.

b. They double the area and interest of view.

c. They insure that on sunny days there will always be some time, regardless of orientation, when the sun will shine within the apartment. This is especially important for retired persons since they spend so many daylight hours at home.

A usual plan is rectangular and has four corners. Early in our studies we crossed two rectangles, resulting in a Greek-cross form that provided eight corners. The final plan we devised, a modified **T** with a cross at each end of the **T** gave us a total of eighteen corner-apartments out of twenty-four, or 75 per cent, an unusual and most beneficial arrangement.

LOCATION

I would guess that the most controversial aspect of elderly housing is its site or location—urban, suburban, or rural. Even within our own organization the views are disparate. We will tabulate the advantages and disadvantages, although it seems fair to note that the choice often relates to the scenes of one's life. Usually, those who have lived in the city most of their lives prefer an urban location; similarly, those who have lived in the country prefer a suburban or rural site. Perhaps it is simply a natural inclination toward the easiest adjustment. Needless to say, the advantages and disadvantages listed below are applicable, in the strict sense of the word, to life care only. A rural location, for all its charm, cannot replace proximity to a grocery store for an aged person living independently, without an automobile.

Urban

Advantages

Convenient to shopping, entertainment, sports, cultural activities.

A dynamic, active environment. Usually closer or more convenient to friends and family.

Disadvantages

Traffic, noise, gas fumes and smog, little exposure to nature (gardens, flowers). Views usually overlooking unpleasant rooftops before encompassing more rewarding distant views.

Rural

Advantages

Quiet, peaceful, the feel of nature. Fresh air, clear sunshine, gardening usually available, golf courses near as well as other country pleasures—walking, fishing and so on. The greatest advantage of a rural location is the opportunity to acquire a much larger parcel of land for a fraction of urban costs, thus permitting generous areas for gardens, terraces, games such as shuffleboard and lawn bowling, and other outdoor pleasure-spaces which cannot be provided on the usual, tight urban site.

Disadvantages

Urban attractions (shopping, sports, culture, and so on) can be experienced only infrequently and often inconveniently.

CONSTRUCTION TYPE

High-rise multistoried buildings are usually built in an urban setting; rambling one- or two-story residential types are most frequently constructed in a suburban or rural setting, although there seems to be an increasing trend toward high-rise buildings located in the country.

The rambling type has three rather severe limitations: (1) it is difficult to achieve open planning for over two-hundred units without adding an unduly long travel or walk between distant units and the central dining areas; (2) except in southwestern or southern climates these covered walkways must be closed and heated in winter; and (3) while a rambling type can be fireproofed, it is usually frame construction, and the trend is toward fireproof construction. Its chief advantage is economy. A residential one- or two-story building is between one half and two thirds the cost of a high-rise building. It is also less institutional in appearance.

SIZE OF PROJECT

There are two limitations affecting the size of a project or the number of apartment units and, consequently, the number of residents. The low limitation is primarily economic. It is evident that as the number of units diminishes, the cost per unit to maintain the same quality and variety of services must increase. For example, the yearly salary of an administrator is the same, whether there are two-hundred or three-hundred units. Thus, that portion of the monthly rental fee assigned to this administrative cost would be 50 per cent more in a two-hundred-unit project. Conversely, less money is thus made available for other services in the two-hundred-unit project. This principle applies to many other items. Much of the administrative costs, some maintenance costs, and all land costs, for example, are approximately the same regardless of the number of units. Hence, the cost borne by each unit is higher when the project contains fewer units.

The high limitation is not, as might be anticipated, also economic, but is estimated to be that number of persons which can live with comfort and dignity in a relationship which is noninstitutional in atmosphere. Admittedly, this is a difficult quality to determine since much of the quality of a pleasant environment is achieved with able and sensitive management. Our experience is that three-hundred units is about the maximal limit.

SPECIAL PLANNING ARRANGEMENTS

General

Most articles about housing for the elderly stress conveniences which are, for the most part, theoretical. In actual practice we have learned that minimal changes from a normal apartment are most appreciated by the elderly. They emphatically do not want to be considered as weak or tired or exhausted; they do not wish special attention or assistance unless they cannot live easily without it.

It is a rare article on planning that does not mention that electrical outlets should be located about table height so that the elderly do not stoop to plug in or change a lamp cord. This sounds eminently practical until we remember that an elderly person may change a lamp outlet, at most, once a month, but will bend further and lower twice a day to put on and take off his shoes. Also note that it is easier to trip over a cord extending from an outlet 30 inches high than from an outlet close to the floor.

For some time, certain codes required a stair riser not over 6 inches high and a tread not less than 12 inches wide, as compared to a more usual 7.5 to 10 inches proportion. The theory was that they were easier for the elderly to travel, although if the floor-to-floor height is constant, the energy spent to climb either is the same. This requirement usually applies only to fire stairs, but in an emergency or in panic conditions, people remember those intervals they have known most of their lives. Thus this change, considered to make the life of the elderly easier, may endanger that life. Certain bath fittings, designed to aid the senile, may affront those who are as active and energetic as are the majority over sixty-two (the minimum age). For example, no one wants side-bars alongside the toilet until physical debility may require them and, at that time, they can be readily installed. Also, it does not seem wise to arrange space and fixtures to accommodate a wheelchair in every bathroom when less than 5 per cent of the residents ever have such need. It is better to provide these special arrangements in a few selected apartments.

All of this is not to say that we should not consider age in our planning. Anything which may ease life without undue comment or attention (such as easy grades and few stairs), of course, should be considered. The important things to avoid are planning-clichés which are impractical or unwise.

Public Areas

Major Spaces

RECEPTION

There should be a generous lobby for visitors, attended by a receptionist, with a small, adjacent visiting-room where residents may receive guests. The receptionist's office should open to both the visitors' lobby and the main lounge. The receptionist also operates the telephone exchange at this location and, in smaller projects, helps with accounting, typing, mailing, or similarly light tasks.

ADMINISTRATIVE

Opening from and connected to the receptionist-PBX space are the administrative offices, usually with separate rooms for the administrator, assistant administrator, and secretary and a general office. These areas are placed to permit easy, casual, and frequent exchanges between residents and management. The administrator's office should have an informal corner with comfortable lounge chairs and a coffee table, designed to ease the sometimes difficult or strained interviews with families or guests at entry. A small shop for the sale of drugs, sundries, cosmetics, newspapers, and magazines is placed near this area, and the post office boxes are also adjacently located since distribution is usually done by administrative personnel.

LOUNGE

A large lounge, connected to elevators or walkways, to the administrative area, and leading to the dining space, is the single, common, everyday meeting area, a place of relaxation and conversation. It must be large enough to accommodate all the residents in comfort since they usually congregate there before and after luncheon and dinner. Sometimes, small informal musicals or talks are held in the lounge and always, after formal concerts in the auditorium, the lounge entertains a delightful meet-the-artist gathering.

DINING ROOM-KITCHEN

The dining room should be a high-ceilinged generous space. In one of the retirement projects this large area was partitioned off with attractive venetian blinds into a series of smaller spaces, on the theory that intimate areas would invest a more informal, less-institutional atmosphere. All was well, until at the first holiday celebration, the blinds were gathered to open the many alcoves into one big space. The residents were so pleased with this change that the areas were never again subdivided. It is extremely easy in the design of elderly-housing to confuse social theory with actual living practices and preferences. At least 15 sq ft per person should be allowed in design, and the dining room should be large enough to accept all residents comfortably at one sitting.

The art of kitchen design has become a highly specialized field with its own association of experts, the International Society of Food Service Consultants. It is axiomatic that restaurant service is no better than its kitchen. It is difficult at best to maintain interesting variety in the daily menu, and a skillfully planned kitchen is essential. It is also important to arrange food service to supply the other daily requirements (medical center and breakfast places), as well as the less-frequent catering to parlors, lounges, or private dining rooms. These more-distant dining areas require the specialized palleting and tray-cart service which such functions use.

The management of one of our projects has shown imagination in relieving a normal dining tedium, whether home or commercial, by varying not only the menu but also the environment. Occasionally on pleasant days and at special times, dinner is held on the terrace or alfresco in the garden, with a Hawaiian luau or western barbecue or eastern-shore steamed dinner. These are the kinds of imaginative touches which minimize the institutional atmosphere so unfortunately common with projects of this kind.

LIBRARY

A library, designed more like a clubroom library than a public library, is most important. The books are best kept on shelves with locked sliding doors, the magazines and daily papers on open tables and racks. Usually, one of the residents enjoys the responsibility of operation. The atmosphere should also resemble a clubroom—dark and cloistered with heavy hangings and deep leather-upholstered chairs. Of all rooms, the library is the best spot for a fireplace—and make it real-wood-burning, not a cheap gas-log imitation.

TELEVISION ROOMS

Public viewing of television is often trying. There is a great, vast, deep, unbridgeable gulf between those who prefer "The Beverly Hillbillies," football games, "Open End," or Lawrence Welk. It is best to provide separate rooms.

HOBBY ROOMS

The retirement-tract type of elderly-housing projects places great stress upon hobby rooms. There are built large and exceptionally well equipped rooms for a multitude of hobbies—weaving, sewing, carpentry, jewelry, painting, ceramics, metalworking, and so on. Time has proved that although many people entertained the idea of devoting the retirement years of their lives to a career in the arts, few made other than sporadic attempts at what should be a serious, albeit pleasant, pursuit. This is not to say that space should not be provided for hobbies; it should. But the residents, through their own action, will determine the type of use and space they may prefer. Usually only those persons who pursued hobbies during their active years continue this interest after retirement.

GALLERY

There are a great number of traveling cultural exhibits which rarely receive popular, interested attention. In several plans we have introduced a small gallery, usually along a well-traveled way, for the showing of these exhibits. This gallery also provides display space for the handicraft and genre artifacts created in the hobby shops. It is also surprising to note how many fine paintings are owned by the residents, who are usually pleased to loan them for a showing. The success of the gallery, the variety of exhibits and displays, rests almost entirely with the management, although the residents council has often taken an abiding interest.

MULTIPURPOSE ROOM

This space should be large enough to seat every resident in auditorium manner. It should have a stage and should be designed to accept easily all the uses to which it may be put and which include, among others, the following: musicals, lectures, plays, concerts, meetings, movies, dances, card games, religious functions, and art shows.

The degree of completeness is a management decision: whether to have impromptu home-movies or a professional booth with two projectors, whether to have full stage-equipment with flies or a small stage without footlights. Whatever policy is adopted, it is important to provide all the equipment and storage space needed to meet that policy. It is also important to realize that as the stage and related facilities become more complex, the added fire-safety requirements disproportionately increase the cost.

Minor Spaces

LOUNGES OR PARLORS

In garden-type projects, "parlors" (in high-rise apartments, "lounges") are provided, convenient to the apartments, for informal, smaller groups, supplementing the major public areas. These smaller areas serve a multitude of uses: they can be reserved and catered for informal family-gatherings, a Thanksgiving dinner or an anniversary; they are meeting-places for the many interest clubs or associations that flourish in this environment. In many centers a continental breakfast is served occasionally to give a change of scene from the dining room; television can be enjoyed; and, last, since the laundry room is usually located adjacent to these parlors or lounges, they are convenient as a place for rest or talk between loads.

LAUNDRIES

Laundries are minimum in size and are used for personal laundry only. Laundry of bed and bathroom linens is usually provided within the monthly fee.

SOLARIUMS

These are most desirable, particularly in the usually congested urban location where exercise and outdoor space is severely limited. In such a setting the solarium is placed on the roof, often with an adjacent outdoor terrace. The rooftop location is usually windy because high-rise building shapes impede normal airflow—directing much of the wind over the top—and suitable windscreens must be provided. When the solarium is correctly oriented and attractively landscaped, it can become one of the most enjoyable, restful places in the entire project.

Operational Spaces

Efficient and economical operation of a project as complex as a retirement residence deserves as much study and research as the public rooms or the apartments. Consider the variety of operation in a typical high-rise retirement project. We have the following:

a. A 150-car garage.

b. A twelve-story apartment house.

c. A three-hundred-seat auditorium.

d. A large dining room with a kitchen larger than that required by an average restaurant.

e. A fifty-five-bed convalescent hospital with x-ray room, darkroom, laboratory, pharmacy, and therapy rooms.

It is obvious from this short recitation of functions that their economic and efficient maintenance, operation, and servicing are wholly dependent upon a thoroughly researched and programmed schedule and that the planning of spaces to accommodate this schedule must be detailed, complete, and correctly sized.

Every day, tons of material are brought in and taken out of this complex. Transport and storage alone can mean a difference in operational costs of several thousand dollars a year. How is trash stored? Is a refrigerated room provided? How close to storage and distribution areas are deliveries arranged? Where are employees' locker rooms and lounges located? What planning can be done to minimize pilferage? Where should the mechanical room be located— in the basement or on the roof? How is the soiled linen from the apartments separated from the hospital linen? The questions are seemingly endless, and there is no simple, straightforward set of answers or easily referenced checklist which can be devised.

Many of the matters of planning are determined by management. For example: Is linen received, checked, and distributed individually from a basement supply-room or is it moved forward on receipt to the various linen-storage closets located on each floor? In the kitchen operation, must provision be made for a bakery or is the management's decision to purchase pastries? How many employees will have meal privileges and where, then, should the employees' dining room be placed? These questions indicate the range of decisions which must be reached, questions which extend beyond the usual, mechanical building-spaces such as telephone rooms, transformer vaults, servicing and repair shops (carpentry, plumbing, heating, painting), boiler rooms, fan rooms, compressor rooms, and so forth which are common to the average structure.

Outdoor Spaces

Terraces

In suburban and rural projects the patios and gardens of the apartments continue without interruption into the public spaces, terraces, and gardens. In urban locations and most suburban sites, the terraces are raised above street level to insure privacy and provide security and insulation against the hazards as well as the traffic and noise of the street. Although a small street-level entrance lobby is provided, all the major public areas occur at the terrace level which becomes, in effect, the first floor. Most of the public rooms (dining, multipurpose, hobby, lounge, and so on) open onto this terrace, and in pleasant weather it becomes an interesting area. Usually, one side is for games and active use, the other for gardens and contemplation. It is very desirable to create delightfully landscaped areas with pools and fountains, gazebos, trees in decorative planters, and flowering ground-covers, to ameliorate the omnipresent cement and asphalt of an urban setting.

Recreation Space

Three games are always popular with the elderly; they are good fun-games and combine pleasure and exercise. The games are shuffleboard, croquet, and lawn bowling. The choice is often limited in urban areas by available space. The sizes quoted below are for the net court-area. American shuffleboard is 52 by 6 ft; English is 40 by 4.5 ft. American croquet is 60 by 30 ft; modern croquet is 85 ft by 37 ft 2 in. A two-alley bowling green is 120 by 40 ft. Two other games, horseshoes or quoits and *boccie* are sometimes played; the first with a court of about 80 by 25 ft, the latter 62 by 18 ft. Medical opinion increasingly turns toward the advocacy of adequate exercise for the elderly, including even those with coronary problems, and an active sports program with resident-council-organized competition is both enjoyable and rewarding. In one project the resident council not only arranged some enjoyable tournaments but picked a championship mens, womens and mixed-doubles team that challenged other retirement centers, a sort of reverse Little League.

In rural projects, vegetable gardens have on some occasions been laid out with individual plots about 20 by 40 ft. They have been plowed, harrowed, and assigned to those interested. Rarely does such interest continue beyond one season. The task of caring for such a plot is at best a taxing experience, and few have the will or stamina to continue. However, almost everyone in a rural site likes to have a tiny garden area of his own, usually part of his patio, sometimes only a few flowerpots or planters where he can grow succulents, flowers, or shrubs. The care of this type of garden is a light, enjoyable hobby followed by many of the residents. At some residences, garden societies or groups pool their common interests, with yearly prizes, lectures, and tours—often directed by local landscape-architects—to nearby private gardens. More-formal gardens, of course, embellish the terraces. These are carefully designed and are maintained by a professional staff of gardeners.

Medical Center

Rooms

It has been common practice for many years to provide almost all rooms of a size which will accommodate two beds. Lately this trend is changing, especially in facilities designed to provide long-term care for the elderly. It is best to provide as many private rooms as possible. Obviously, this is more expensive. With rapidly increasing labor-costs, however, the importance of the cost of construction is proportionately less. Almost all states spell out in exact detail the size of beds; spaces between beds, and between beds and walls; type of curtains and tracks; travel-distance between nurses' station and rooms; kinds of video and audio controls, and a host of other code requirements. These requirements must of course be consulted and must govern. Incidentally, a most excellent and authoritative selection of information on nursing homes and hospitals is available from the Public Health Service.

The programing we describe will cover generally only those subjects not limited by code. The number of baths, as in private homes, is increasing. Today we usually provide a bath for each two-bed room, and a shared toilet between two single rooms with lavatories in the rooms themselves.

Room Furnishings

Television is a must, and in a two-bed room, two televisions are desirable. They must be operated from the bed. In one hospital which we inspected in Boston, small Sony televisions were installed with a scissor aerial attached to the headboard. It permitted easy, inexpensive, direct control; minimum sound levels; and simple, convenient adjustment and servicing. The best (and as usual, most expensive) beds lower electrically to a comfortable residence-type bed height. For work by the nurses (rubbing, bathing, changing linen) the bed is electrically elevated. In addition, it also electrically changes head- and knee-positions. All these devices—television, bed, as well as audiovisual devices—are controlled by the patient from a natural-wood-finished console-type table.

Medical centers in contemporary retirement residences are being decorated in a homelike rather than hospital style. More and more attention is given to warm, friendly details. For example, bedsteads, instead of the usual, white-painted, wrought-iron hospital cot, have natural-wood-grained head- and footboards. Pleasant wall colors, beautifully designed washable wall covering, painted acoustical tile ceilings, shaded lighting fixtures: many are the ways in which the rooms are made more livable and more restful. Carpeting has become commonplace, and experience has proven that over the life of the structure, carpets may be more hygienic and economical. (If carpeting is selected, it is best to consult state hospital-codes as to mandatory bacterial tests.)

Public Spaces

The entrance, whether by elevator or separate lobby, should adjoin the nurses' station in a manner which insures full and constant supervision. Many of the residents in the medical facility are in a so-called twilight zone. They may require help in dressing or eating, they may become forgetful, but they are definitely not bed patients. These people sometimes tend to wander, and control of the exits is necessary to limit their adventuring. In addition, it is important, of course, to have a supervised control center for visitors and guests. Corridors should be a minimum of eight feet wide with a handrail on at least one side, preferably on two.

The nurses' station, the nerve center and control center, must be as efficient as modern science. All records, communications systems, drugs, and supplies must be easily accessible. This center consists of the nurses' station, an open counter for access and surveillance, the head nurse's office with adjacent toilet and dressing room, the clean-linen room, the soiled-linen room, the medicine closet, pantry, and the utility room.

Care must be taken to provide locks for patients' medicine storage as well as storage for internal and external medicines. Double locks, of course, must be provided for narcotics. Such precautions are especially important in long-term-care facilities where patients may be inclined to wander. It may be said that this danger is lessened in a well-staffed facility. Nonetheless, it is not uncommon for both night nurses (in a twenty-five-bed facility) to be occupied with one patient while the remaining patients are assumed to be sleeping. The procedure for narcotic control, of course, varies from state to state. A new trend is toward including a pharmacy in the long-term-care facilities—an entirely new operational problem.

Space must be provided for the storage of gurneys and folded wheelchairs. Baths with tubs free on three sides with lifting and lowering equipment are mandatory, as well as separate, oversized showers large enough to accommodate wheelchairs. If patients are to be left alone in the bathtub, alarms must be provided, and locked cabinets for cleaning solvents must be accessible to the nurse.

In the medical facility, at or near the entrance and also under the nurses' supervision and direction, is located the doctor's office for the internist or general practitioner who cares for all of the residents. This space is divided as is a typical doctor's-clinic with reception room, one and preferably two examination rooms, and the doctor's office or consultation room, with adjacent private toilet and dressing rooms. Because of the slower reactions of the elderly we are generous in the allocation of both space and number in dressing rooms.

Day Room-Dining Area

The day room-dining area is also decorated in a friendly, informal style. In European, especially Scandinavian, projects for the elderly, particular stress is laid on investing this room with a homelike character. Part of the problem with many patients is a gradually diminishing awareness, and the more restful the environment, the easier and more gentle is the adjustment and care. Those who are unable to leave their rooms are served in bed, but it is important to urge all who are able, to attend the dining room meals.

Therapy

Physical and mental therapy are increasingly employed. The entire subject, bound as it is with great lack in the knowledge of mental and chemical treatment of the aging, is nevertheless rapidly progressing. Planning for rehabilitation should include mental, physical- and hydro-therapy; occupational therapy; exercise areas; speech center with appropriate electronic aids; and crafts and tools employed to redevelop dexterity. As previously noted, the Public Health Service has many excellent pamphlets on the subject of rehabilitation.

Visiting Rooms

A minimum of two small rooms, furnished in simple homelike style, is necessary for guests and family visits. Sometimes these visits are trying to both sides; sometimes they are pleasant and friendly. It is important to provide privacy, the privacy of your own home, for these occasions.

Parking

The ratio of required parking spaces to apartments varies according to the following factors:

    a. Location of project. A rural project will obviously have a higher parking-apartment ratio than one located in the heart of a city.

b. Economic level of residents. A higher economic level also has an obviously higher car ownership ratio than a welfare or low-income project.

c. Average age of residents or project. The age of the residents has the most direct bearing on the project. Those projects with long operating histories have the lowest ratio and average about 13 per cent parking spaces to total apartments.

Management makes every effort to discourage driving because of the hazards, even in rural locations. Limousine service is usually provided in spite of increasing costs. This is done because of the physical limitations of the residents—poor vision, lowered hearing levels, slower reflexes—the infirmities characteristic of old age. Of importance, also, is the cost of owning a car, which amounts to some twelve hundred dollars per year, plus the high cost of providing space.

As a general rule of thumb, we usually provide 50 per cent parking spaces (ratio .5:1), although it varies by project, as initially stated. In areas where the ratio cannot be readily determined, or where local planning officials are uncertain of demand, a reasonable projection can often be made from a careful analysis of the first 20 to 30 per cent of actual apartment sales.

Regulatory Agencies

As our society grows increasingly complex we sometimes think that our regulatory agencies increase not in arithmetical but in geometric ratio. A short time ago one of our clients remarked about one of the conflicts between the codes of two overlapping regulations, and, more in sorrow than in anger, we compiled a list of regulations on housing for the elderly. This particular project was in California, but we hasten to add that California is not unchallenged in its intricacy. Some of the various hazards which confront the architect reviewing these agencies and regulations are as follows:

a. In the event of conflict, the more rigid regulation governs.

b. Some of the restrictions are written in language so turgid that even those governmental specialists involved argue the interpretation among themselves.

c. Many of the regulations provide specifically for local interpretation. This will vary from place to place.

d. Some of the agencies are obscure. I recall one whose influence and restrictive control was not discovered until late in the preliminary studies, necessitating radical plan-changes and time loss.

e. The time required to obtain some governmental approvals can be costly, particularly if land must be optioned during that time. One of our zoning applications required twenty-three separate appearances over an eleven-month period before approval was secured.

In addition to the basic requirement of studying these regulations in depth, and the vagaries of enforcement and conflict, there remains the final vexing problem of frequent change, amendment, or revision of regulations. The aforementioned list follows:

Governmental Regulations which Impose Restrictions or Controls over Elderly Housing

A. Subdivided Lands
   1. California Business and Professions Code
B. Master Plan
   1. County or city
C. Zoning Regulations and Ordinances
   1. County or city
D. Building Requirements
   1. Uniform Building Code
   2. Local variations of UBC (These can run from ten to 500 pages.)
   3. Local building code (a separate code unrelated to UBC as in San Francisco)
E. Building Code Standards

   These vary from the concise 511-page small-print UBC compilation to the 122 separate pamphlets referenced in the Fire Safety Code. We again refer to the problems with these obscure agencies and regulations because a requirement contained in any of these hundreds of pages of standards is just as enforceable as a requirement spelled out in the basic code.
F. Manual of Institutions for Aged Persons, Department of Social Welfare

G. Hospital Licensing Act and Requirements, Department of Public Health

H. Requirements to meet the standards of Medicare, including but not limited to, the Joint Commission of Hospital Accreditation, American Hospital Association and statewide hospital-associations. Some are mandatory, others are not.

I. Requirements where Women are Employed, Department of Industrial Relations

J. Fire and Safety Standards, Title 19, Public Safety—California Adm. Code

K. Elevator Safety Orders, Division of Industrial Safety

L. State Housing Act, Division of Housing

M. Earthquake Protection Law, Division of Housing

N. Plumbing Code
   1. National or local

O. Electrical Code
   1. National or local

P. General Industrial Safety Orders, Department of Industrial Relations

The checker in our office concerned with these regulations estimated, from idle curiosity, the number of words in these laws; the total: an astounding 13.5 million.

Section Two
The *Pro Forma*

Chapter I

AN INTRODUCTION TO THE *PRO FORMA*

Estimating the criteria of operations for an elderly housing project involves the interrelation of many factors, all of which are necessary in the realization of the end result of a cost analysis—the profit or loss on the project. Our method of analysis, listed below, is the result of a wide experience range. It has been developed for two basic purposes:

    a. To provide a method of developing accurate cost projections for the original analysis.

    b. To provide a frame of reference from which will emerge a simple and direct method of cost accounting which will allow a subsequent review by management and the later comparison in detail with other operations to detect any imbalance that may develop.

THE PROJECT SUMMARY

The project summary is prepared to permit accurate forecasting of certain costs and certain factors necessary to project the annual statement. It includes, for example, the total replacement cost—a cost required to determine entrance fees, annual taxes, insurance, and so on. It also includes the square footage of individual apartments with their space related by per cent to the total apartment areas. This will establish a guide to proportion the cost of entrance fees equally. Total square-foot costs, number of apartments, and number of residents are likewise essential in the annual statement, since many of these factors relate to units employed in developing such costs as laundry, food, heating, and so forth. Thus it may be seen that the project summary, while not directly utilized in the annual statement, is absolutely essential in providing initial costs or unit factors for such use.

THE ANNUAL STATEMENT

The annual statement estimates or forecasts the expected income (including a vacancy percentage); the operating, maintenance, dietary, medical and replacement-reserves annual costs; the taxes; and the debt service. The income minus the costs leaves, of course, the surplus or loss. Since these projects are usually operated on a nonprofit basis there could not normally be an allowance set aside for income or corporate taxes.

While little reference is made to the design of the project, it is obvious that certain design elements should be carefully evaluated. This subject is treated at some length in another chapter, but it should be noted that the quality of construction and the directly related maintenance costs must be carefully weighed. For example, How much insulation should be installed? The obvious answer, which is so often overlooked, is, that amount on which the cost will be less on a long-term amortized basis than the savings in the cost of the heating and cooling which it will gain. However, since many excellent books have been written on the subject of design, we limit our observations only to that area where design may have a marked influence on operating costs.

Chapter II

COSTS OF DEVELOPMENT

PROJECT SUMMARY

THE DETAILED LISTING of ratios, square-foot areas, number of residents, entrance fees, and monthly fees, provides a ready and convenient reference table that is frequently employed in computing costs in the annual statement. From these detailed listings we may determine laundry or food costs (per person), heating costs (on either a net or gross square-foot basis), rent income (per apartment unit), and so on. A form for these listings is shown in Appendix A. A few comments pertaining to each heading follow:

Type

This describes, by shorthand, the exact kind of apartment unit. Rather than "studio apartment," "one-bedroom," and so on, we have used a system followed by a number as giving a more exact description. This we begin with a one-unit apartment, A1, which describes a living-room-bedroom common area, adjacent bath and closets, with built-in kitchenette. A single-unit apartment A2 has the same accommodations, only larger. A one-and-one-half-unit apartment Ba1 would contain a living room with an alcove off the living room for a bed space that can be closed off from the living room by a sliding door, a bath adjacent to the alcove, closet space, and a kitchenette off the living room—in effect, a small one-bedroom apartment. This arrangement, incidentally, is by far the most popular of all apartments, combining economy and flexibility. One-and-one-half-unit apartments Ba2, Ba3, or Ba4 would likewise indicate increasingly larger areas in similar types. A two-unit apartment B has a living room with kitchenette, separate bedroom and bath, and required closets. A three-unit apartment C, the same, except with two bedrooms, and so on.

This system is also used with the life-care sales plans and floor plans and later related to the management and location plan with a number preceding the unit description which locates the placement of the unit on the floor and the floor level (fourth, fifth, and so on). Thus an identifying reference system is initially adopted which is uniform throughout construction, leasing, accounting, and operations.

Total Unit Rooms

In developing comparisons between various projects, a ratio of the average number of rooms per apartment is most equitable. Our factor is based on the following count:

Studio apartment	1 room
Alcove apartment	1½ rooms
One-bedroom apartment	2 rooms
Two-bedroom apartment	3 rooms

This figure reflects a management policy decision usually reached before the architectural planning is started. Two obvious axioms are pertinent:

a. The lower the average income of the expected residents, the higher the percentage of one- and one-and-one-half-unit apartments.

b. The higher the percentage of one- and one-and-one-half-unit apartments, the higher will be the construction cost per square foot, since the expensive elements (bath, kitchen, balcony) are the same whether in one-, one-and-one-half-, two-, or three-unit apartments.

Apartments—Single, Double, Total

The total number of each type is a simple mathematical computation. However, the allocation of the per cent of single and double occupancy of these units is judged solely on our operating experience in the income group for whom the building has been designed.

Residents—per Unit, Total

These two columns of the project summary are used to determine the number of residents per apartment type and the total resident population. This, likewise, is a simple projection of the apartment division except for the original management policy decision on the various apartment sizes and on the number of couples (married, sisters, friends, or brothers) who will need double accommodations. This usually runs about 1.15 persons per apartment at the time of opening, with a larger ratio of couples occupying the larger apartments. The average density of all life-care projects on the West Coast is 1.14, which reflects the eventual and inevitable decrease in density.

Entrance Fees—per Unit, Total

The foregoing four columns develop the information needed in computing the entrance fees. In the usual retirement project there are many facilities provided such as dining room, kitchen, multipurpose room, hobby rooms, medical center, and so on. The cost of these facilities must be included, of course, in the financing of the entire project, and the most equitable method of doing this is through a determination of what part or per cent an individual apartment bears in relation to the whole. These fees should normally total about 70 per cent of the total replacement cost, and about five sevenths should be applied against replacement costs.

Monthly Fees—per Month, per Year, Total

The total monthly-fee income is applied against the total operating costs. It is important to separate both entrance fees and monthly fees into single- and double-occupancy apartment-cost assignments. In standard apartments the operating-cost differential between one or two persons occupying the same apartment is negligible. However, in housing for our elders, additional items are included in the monthly maintenance costs (such as meals, linen, medical care, and so on) which have a definite reflection in operating costs if an apartment is occupied by one or two persons. This comprises the total apartment income. Any other rental income, such as garage and shops, should, of course, be added in the space provided to indicate the gross income available. We repeat, however, that the project summary is basically only a ready table of statistics to which all subsequent analyses are referenced.

CONSTRUCTION ESTIMATE

It is important to realize and to understand fully that the cost of construction of an elderly-housing project and the subsequent financing and debt service are not as dominant factors as they usually are in a more standard project. As will be later detailed, a 10 per cent savings, for example, in the construction cost in an elderly-housing project will equal only a 4.5 per cent decrease in debt service and that, in turn, will reduce the total operating cost by scarcely 1 per cent. Not infrequently a 10 per cent cost reduction involves a substitution of inferior elements or products which may so increase maintenance costs that the theoretical 1 per cent savings is wiped out. In fact, so-called savings in some areas may actually require an increase in total income. Further, a 10 per cent decrease in construction cost only reduces the entrance fees about 6.5 per cent. Last, since the entire project could be normally retired after a ten to twenty-year period, it is obvious that during that period and thereafter, both the sponsors and the occupants would lose in every way from a cheaply built project.

This does not, of course, condone waste or extravagance, but it does mean that those elements which contribute to pleasant living— soundproofing between apartments, air conditioning, kitchenettes, well-conceived gardens and landscaping, piping of adequate size, sufficient lighting outlets (all of the areas that so frequently are either skimpy or shoddy in so much of today's speculative construction)—should be and, economically, must be well designed and well constructed.

ESTIMATED DEVELOPMENT COST

Land Improvements
    Off-site $_____
    On-site
        Utilities   _____
        Parking area   _____
        Sidewalks   _____
        Landscaping   _____
        Demolition
        Site preparation   _____
        Other   _____
           Total Land Improvements $_____

Construction

Item	Sq Ft	Cost Sq Ft	Total
-------	-------	-------	-------
-------	-------	-------	-------
-------	-------	-------	-------
-------	-------	-------	-------
-------	-------	-------	-------
-------	-------	-------	-------

Total Construction $_____

Total for Construction and Land
    Improvement $_____

Fees
  Builder's general overhead
    $_____ @ _____% $_____
  Builder's profit
    $_____ @ _____%   _____
  Architect-engineer's fee
    $_____ @ _____%   _____
  Soils eng.—surveys _____%   _____
    Total Fees $_____
    Total for all Improvements $_____

Carrying Charges_____
  Interest _____ mos. @ _____% on
    $_____ $_____
  Taxes during construction (land only)   _____
  Insurance
    Fire   _____
    Liability   _____
    Property damage   _____
    Builders risk   _____
    Fidelity bond   _____
    Bond premium   _____
  Other   _____
    Total Carrying Charges $_____

Financing
  Mortgage fees
    Insurance premiums $_____
    Examination fee   _____
    Inspection fee   _____
  Financing expense   _____
  Title and recording   _____
  Other   _____
    Total Financing Costs $_____

Legal and Organization
  Legal $_____
  Organization   _____
  Advertising   _____
  Sales promotion   _____
  Other   _____
    Total Legal and Organization $_____

Land
  _____ @ $_____ $_____
    Total Estimated Development Cost $_____

There are as many ways of computing development or replacement costs as there are of figuring square-foot areas. In our method we start with what we call "bare-bones" costs, or the total cost of the project to the contractor of the building on the site. This includes off-site costs, on-site costs, and job overhead. To this are added all construction fees (which include builder's general or office overhead, and builder's profit) and architect and engineer's fees (including soils, mechanical, electrical, kitchen equipment, structural, and civil engineering). This gives a total for the base cost of all improvements. To this are added the following:

    a. Carrying charges. This factor includes the interest during construction, the taxes during construction, and the insurance (fire, liability, property, builder's risk, fidelity, bond).

    b. Financing. This includes mortgage fees, insurance premiums, examination fees, inspection fees, and title and recording costs.

    c. Legal and organizational. This heading embraces all those costs necessary or required to initiate the project and includes legal fees, organization costs, advertising and the related sales and sales promotion (a major item).

The final cost to add is the cost of the land. This includes all legal and required closing costs; options; interest payments; and rezoning costs if required, and they usually are. As a safety factor we usually add an additional 5 per cent contingency to these preliminary estimated costs. This concludes all of the estimated development costs.

Architects and contractors usually have checklists to insure the reasonable completeness of the project. For example, off-site costs might require the construction of new utilities to serve the property. On-site costs may include items such as sidewalks, landscaping, demolition, site clearing or preparation, parking, storm-drains, and underground wiring. Our office has a detailed eleven-page requirements list for on- and off-site work, with separate pages for surveys, drainage, roads and parking, sewerage, trash removal, domestic water supply, gas, electricity, telephone, postal service, and codes. These are further subdivided in detail; for example, under "Surveys," the subheads of Boundary Survey (easements, right-of-way, boundaries), Topographical Survey (with existing structures, trees, rock outcroppings, prevailing-wind direction, views, and so forth), and Utility Survey are listed. Construction costs may include local or state agency fees, and so on. In any event, it is extremely important that experienced and responsible people be retained or employed for this highly complex and important part of the total project.

Frequently there are savings which can be made by prior arrangement. Title and recording costs, for instance, first of land and, later, land and structure for mortgage purposes, can often be so arranged or combined that the usual total of the separate fees is not demanded.

Obviously the entire field of development cost is fraught with difficulties, problems, and opportunities which require for conception and execution the knowledge and talents of many highly trained persons; it is not a field for the inexperienced.

Chapter III

INTRODUCTION TO THE ESTIMATE OF ANNUAL OPERATING COSTS

O PERATING COSTS are most accurately divided into five categories:
1. Administrative.
2. Operating.
3. Maintenance.
4. Dietary.
5. Medical.

The divisions within these categories are listed according to the recommended *pro forma* statement which, of necessity, lists items alphabetically rather than by financial or managerial importance.*

This work is concerned with economics. It was not intended to suggest operating or administrative procedures. Nor was it intended as a discussion of moral and social values. Still, by nature, the economics of housing for the aged is inseparable from such values, and operating and administrative procedures must be defined to understand certain costs. Perhaps this is the fascination as well as the challenge to management—the ever-present dichotomy of cost as opposed to quality.

---

*For the sake of cross-reference, category numbers are maintained within each division. For example: Reference to 3.2 will designate Category 3, item 2 on Maintenance—Furniture and Furnishings.

Chapter IV

ESTIMATE OF ANNUAL OPERATING COSTS

CATEGORY 1—ADMINISTRATIVE COSTS

1.0	Advertising	$ _____
1.1	Audit	_____
1.2	Automotive	_____
1.3	Fidelity Bond	_____
1.4	General Office Expense, Licenses, Stationery, Association Membership Dues, and so on	_____
1.5	Legal	_____
1.6	Telephone	_____
1.7	Traveling Expenses	_____
1.8	Administrative Payroll	_____
1.9	Other	_____
	Total Administrative	$ _____

1.0 Advertising

ADVERTISING IS A study in itself. Its cost will depend upon the number of residents on the waiting list or the number and nature of vacancies. Generally a straightforward brochure describing the project and the services is the best approach. If it is necessary to generate inquiries the medium used will depend upon the following:

a. Location of the residence or the tenancy market in the immediate area.

b. Sponsoring corporation. (For example: Is it an operation with strong religious restrictions? Or is it an operation that is truly nondenominational?)

c. Economic level of potential residents. This section is concerned with operations and not development. Nonetheless, the experience of developmental advertising is the basis of operational advertising.

1.1 Audit

This is self-explanatory. Needless to say, however, an astute CPA firm can predict inevitable financial problems that may be years away. Many states have laws relative to the frequency and type of audit.

It is advisable, of course, to adapt the accounting procedure to the state audit procedures if possible.

1.2 Automotive

This classification refers to administrative automobiles. It does not refer to transportation for the residents (item 2.6) or to maintenance of vehicles (3.6). As such, it is an operations decision essentially and will vary with the circumstances of the project as to whether or not the administrator or any of his staff are supplied with an automobile as a fringe benefit.

1.3 Fidelity Bond

In any retirement residence, large amounts of money are by necessity handled by the administrative staff. Not only moneys in the sense of receivables, but sometimes in a custodial sense. For example, the transfer of an incompetent resident to a hospital or nursing home may sometimes illustrate the latter instance. The death of a resident and the protection of his properties is another instance. For a residence with over two hundred residents a $50,000 fidelity bond is a minimum. The actual cost of such a bond is comparatively negligible. In some states the amount of the bond is defined by law.

1.4 General Office Expense

This is the cost of office supplies, licenses, stationery, association membership dues, and so on. It is not dissimilar to that of any hotel or hospital. Nonetheless it is advisable to consult state regulations as to required forms. In the State of California, for instance, all forms required by law must be approved by the State Department of Social Welfare as a condition of licensing.

1.5 Legal

The importance of retaining the best available legal counsel cannot be overstressed. Housing for the aged involves a specialty that goes beyond the scope of knowledge of an attorney in general practice. In addition to problems concerned with corporate law, regulatory agencies, and tax law, a typical residence for the aged is confronted with many inherent liabilities. While a great many problems are overcome by competent management and diligent planning, there is nonetheless an impressive amount of legal work. A legal retainer of $5,000 per year for a life-care residence housing three hundred persons would not be unreasonable.

1.6 Telephone

This refers to administrative telephones, not telephones in the residence (2.08). In addition to telephones for the members of the administrative staff, we must not forget telephones for:

a. Housekeeping department.
b. Maintenance department.
c. Medical department.
d. Dietary department.
e. Multipurpose areas.
f. House phone.

Each of the foregoing admits of many variations depending upon the layout of the building as well as the general plan of operations. Sometimes there are supplementary administrative communication costs: In one of our projects, which is a campus-style development spread over many acres, certain key personnel have experimented with small walkie-talkie instruments so they can be reached immediately. Walkie-talkie instruments in a high-rise building are far more complex and often involve special licensing problems.

1.7 Traveling Expenses

This is, essentially, the cost of traveling expenses for the administrator. It covers the costs of attending meetings, conferences, and so on. Although it is a small item from the standpoint of cost, it is an important item from an administrative standpoint. The field of gerontology is expanding at a greater rate than ever before; it is necessary that the administrator keep abreast of new ideas and changing concepts. Certainly the many conferences available throughout the United States and Europe are an excellent medium.

1.8 Administrative Payroll

The administrative payroll will be discussed according to job classification. Union jurisdiction and its economic effect upon management will be considered under Category 2 (Operating Costs) since relatively few union jurisdictions encompass administrative (or clerical) classifications.

Administrator

To thoroughly understand the contemporary role of the administrator, we must examine his work in an historical light. The evolution of housing for the aged as an environment of health and at least some vitality corresponds to the increased emphasis of the importance of the administrator.

Not many years ago the administrator of a home for the aged worked in an unpleasant atmosphere. He was provided with an apartment and food and paid a small salary; his wife helped around the facility and eventually became the "assistant manager." (She received a smaller compensation or none at all.) In other words, the profession attracted men who were idealists, happy to serve a losing cause, or second-rate managers whose lack of ambition compounded an already effete atmosphere. Eventually, sponsoring corporations realized that this practice was poor economy. The importance of the aged as a growing social group, legislation which enacted governmental financing programs, and the increased interest of nonprofit sponsoring groups, warranted a reappraisal of the administrative function. It was obvious that what was true of industry and business was true of housing for the aged; namely, to attract first-rate talent it was necessary to pay well and provide incentives. (The exceptions which stand apart are persons who are members of religious organizations whose contributions now as in the past are redoubtable.)

The many duties of an administrator could be listed, but since this work deals essentially with economics, such a list would be cumbersome. It is enough to say that his duties are multitudinous in a profession brimming with problems. He must be an excellent executive with a thorough knowledge of hospital techniques. Above all, he must be a humanist with deeply rooted ethics and a genuine concern for our elders, with a thorough knowledge of sociology.

To attract such a person it is necessary to pay him a good starting salary. In the San Francisco Bay area our administrators are paid a starting salary of between $12,000 and $15,000 per year. It is necessary, of course, to calculate a graduated increase in salary according to experience and performance. Eventually, the experience of such a man should return every dollar invested.

Administrative Assistant

The administrative assistant is well described by his title. Often he or she is a person in training for an administrator's position. Our firm estimates such a training program as requiring from one to four years, depending upon prior experience. As such, his duties will generally vary according to the operating technique of the administrator. An interesting expansion of this position is to include the responsibility for recreation and program. The effective generation of program (from within the population of the residence) is one of the factors which distinguish a home for our elders from a hotel with a hospital.

Accountant and Assistant Accountant

No job description is necessary here. Needless to say, the accountant should have some CPA experience and relate his work to that of the outside audit firm. On our projects we have been extremely careful in selecting an accountant and usually begin interviewing some months before the actual operation commences. The accounting system should be centralized if the sponsor is operating more than one facility. Centralization allows for the effective use of data-processing equipment (which is essential under Medicare) and a higher-salaried chief accountant.

Stenographer and/or Clerk-Typist

Whether or not a stenographer is necessary depends upon the project. If possible, a clerk-typist is a less costly solution.*

In addition to labor costs, fringe benefits such as those listed below must be considered:

a. Workmen's Compensation Insurance.

---

*Operating, maintenance, dietary and medical payrolls will be discussed in items 2.8, 3.8, 4.8 and 5.8, respectively.

b. State disability insurance.

c. Federal Insurance Compensation Act (FICA).

d. Federal Unemployment Insurance.

e. Hospitalization.

f. Accidental death and dismemberment insurance.

g. Retirement plan.

h. Meals.

i. Vacation plan.

j. Sick leave.

Some of these are compulsory; others are administrative decisions. Some are union requirements; others are state law. They vary widely and increase yearly. An average estimate for fringe benefits today would be about 16 per cent. Unfortunately, a detailed labor-cost breakdown is impossible in that costs vary from location to location to an extent that what is valid in one area would be grossly misleading in another.

CATEGORY 2—OPERATING COSTS

2.0	Utilities		$_____
	2.01 Air Conditioning	$_____	
	2.02 Cooking	_____	
	2.03 Heating	_____	
	2.04 Hot Water	_____	
	2.05 Lighting and Miscellaneous Electric	_____	
	2.06 Elevator Power	_____	
	2.07 Sewer	_____	
	2.08 Telephone	_____	
	2.09 Water	_____	
2.1	Garbage and Trash Removal		
2.2	Housekeeping		_____
	2.20 Housekeeping Materials	_____	
	2.21 Housekeeping Equipment	_____	
2.3	Janitor Materials		
2.4	Laundry and Cleaning		_____
2.5	Linen Replacement		_____
2.6	Resident Transportation		_____
2.7	Window Cleaning		_____
2.8	Operating Payroll		_____
2.9	Other		_____
	Total Operating		$_____

2.0 Utilities

2.01 Air Conditioning

Assuming air conditioning to be necessary there will be variables in the cost projection according to the following:

a. Climatic conditions.

b. Utility rates.

c. Building type (high-rise, single-story, and so on).

d. Architectural design.

e. Mechanical design.

f. Construction.

g. Space requirements (especially nonapartment usage).

With these variables in mind, we shall quote an estimate for one of our large projects which is located in Marin County, north of San Francisco:

a. Air-conditioning auxiliaries, blowers, pumps,
and so forth: 150 kw $\times$ \$.015 per kwh
$\times$ 24 hr $\times$ 365 days $\qquad$ = \$19,600 per annum

b. Air-conditioning compressors: 500 kw
$\times$ 1000 full-load refrigeration hr
per year equivalent $\qquad$ = 7,500
Total a. plus b. $\qquad$ = \$27,100 per annum

This estimate is for a high-rise building. The refrigeration load is due to solar loads and ventilation rates and the factors necessary to regulate the per cent of humidity in the building.

If it is decided that air conditioning or circulation is not necessary in the apartments, its requirement in other areas of the project may be mandatory under law. This is particularly true with laws enacted to diminish the spread of respiratory germs.

2.02 Cooking

Sometimes it is necessary to distinguish between fuel for cooking and fuel for general utility use. Generally this is due to the following:

a. Fuel costs may be part of the dietary contract if the service is contracted.

b. In certain instances the demand during meal periods may exceed the normal utility schedule, thereby increasing costs. This cost varies by area costs, but for the sake of example, may be calculated as follows:

Assume: Electrical fuel with 100 kw of commercial cooking.

Assume: 640 meals per day with the heaviest demand at lunch and dinner.

Assume: An average cost of .015 per kwh.

Therefore, based upon the above assumptions and a projection of 232 kwh during the course of the day, the cost of fuel for cooking is $3.48 per day or about .5 cent per meal.

While the above serves an illustrative purpose, it should not be taken literally since utility costs are frequently in excess of .015 per kwh or its gas fuel equivalent. As a rule of thumb, $5 per resident per year (taking into account absenteeism) is a safe budget figure in the San Francisco Bay area, for example.

2.03 *Heating*

Heating costs are almost impossible to estimate with true accuracy. They vary according to season and geographical area. It is important to know that since the metabolism rate slows with age, it requires a higher room temperature to maintain comfort in these projects. Our design level is usually 75°. Although only 3° above usual practice, this often requires a considerable increase in sizing of heating equipment except in the Southwest and Florida.

Heating costs vary according to space requirements. They are influenced by architectural design and by the craft of construction. The example shown below illustrates some of these variations, that is, season, location, and, to an extent, utility rates. For comparative purposes, the averages used were projected on a 250-apartment, 1.15-density basis with normal nonapartment spaces. Heating costs for hospital buildings were deleted. In each instance the least expensive fuel was assumed, that is, electricity in the Pacific Northwest and gas in the San Francisco Bay area.

VARIATION PER MONTH ON COST OF HEATING FOR 250-UNIT LIFE-CARE PROJECT
(Including Hot Water and Space Heating)

Month	San Francisco Bay Area	Pacific Northwest Area
January	$1,700	$2,250
February	1,400	2,000
March	1,700	1,750
April	1,100	1,550
May	1,000	1,050
June	950	800
July	800	500
August	800	500
September	800	750
October	750	1,000
November	1,400	1,750
December	1,550	2,050

In estimating heating costs it is well to remember certain advantages to high-rise construction due to minimal roof, exterior exposed wall, and floor heat losses. On the other hand, the high fresh-air ventilation rate imposes atypical loads if compared to typical multi-family housing. This type of control requires the continual operation of large blowers, pumps, and other apparatus. We have avoided touching upon the controversy of electric *versus* gas heating. Either may be used successfully.

2.04 Hot Water

This item refers to heating of hot water for domestic purposes and is usually included under 2.03.

2.05 Lighting and Miscellaneous Electrical

This cost is greater in housing for our elders than in typical multi-family residences. Aside from normal appliance usage, apartment lighting is greater due to the visual characteristics of the elderly. More important, however, is the light necessary for multipurpose rooms, outdoor areas, and dietary, medical, and service areas. Such costs will vary somewhat according to season. The most distinct variance in projects studied as well as our own projects is 68 per cent of the highest month.

2.06 Elevator Power

The cost of elevator power is based upon frequency of use. The method of arriving at this cost is best described by example, if 4 kw will power an elevator one mile, assume the following:

a. The elevator will travel at 300 feet per minute.
b. There will be three active periods per day.
c. Each active period equals 3 hours.
d. Cost per kwh: $0.015.

The active-period formula is as follows:

Travel Speed per Minute		Length of Period		No. of Periods		Percent of Operation		Minutes per Hour		No. of Linear Ft. per Elevator
300	×	3	×	3	×	75	×	60	=	121,500

The nonactive-period formula is as follows:

15% of active period or:
15% of 121,500 linear feet   =   18,225

Active and nonactive   =   139,725

139,725 linear feet = approximately 26.5 miles.
26.5 miles × 4 kw per mile = 106 kwh per elevator per day.
$0.015 × 106 kw = $1.59 per elevator per day.
$1.59 × 365 = $580.35 per elevator per year.

2.07 Sewer

Sometimes a city or county will levy a direct sewer charge. This is an area cost and is readily obtainable from the particular district in which the project is located.

2.08 Telephone

The cost of resident telephone service, like most costs in a home for our elders, depends upon what services are offered. Assuming, for example, that emergency calls are by means other than telephone: Will the telephone service consist of a house phone on each floor or in each building complex and a public telephone for outside calls? Or will it consist of a telephone in each apartment with all local calls free? Will the switchboard be open twenty-four hours per day? Let us examine the possibilities from which management may choose:

a. No telephone (or telephone at resident's expense).
b. House telephone only.
c. House telephone with a charge for outside calls.
d. Telephone for in-house and outside calls free, except for long distance.

Obviously, solutions *a, b,* and *c* are, from an economic standpoint, the most practical. Solution d, while the most costly, is the most desirable. In a residence for three hundred persons, however, this item can run as high as $24,000, not including the cost of telephone operators.

If a PBX (private branch exchange) board is used, it will generally require from 2.8 to 3.0 full-time operators and rely on the night watchman and nurse to successively operate the board from midnight until morning. In some projects, a switchboard operator is provided twenty-four hours per day, seven days per week; on others, sixteen hours per day, seven days a week, with relief (as mentioned above) from other departments. A switchboard operator has a second function, that is, as a buffer between residents and management. Residents have questions and problems, and sometimes they just want to talk to someone. Many of these questions can be answered by the switchboard operator and save costly administrative time.

Before a decision is made, it is essential for management to find out if a message unit rate is applicable to the service area of the project. If so, limits on free telephone calls may be in order.

2.09 Water

Actually this cost should be considered from the following two aspects:

a. Water for domestic use, including dietary department, and so forth.

b. Water for landscaping and the maintenance of outdoor areas.

Domestic water consumption will run lower than typical multi-family housing due to the low density factor prevalent in life-care residences. The greatest variance—other than in utility rates—will be according to the amount of landscaped area. Let us compare two examples:

a. Project A is an urban project with minimal landscaping.

b. Project B is a campus-style project with extensive landscaping.

WATER CONSUMPTION
(Based upon 250 Units, 1.2 Density)

Month	Project A High-rise Minimal Garden Area (100 cu ft)	Project B Suburban Extensive Garden Areas (100 cu ft)
January	465	1,715
February	420	1,260
March	380	1,510
April	560	1,477
May	580	2,160
June	570	2,572
July	757	3,025
August	735	3,110
September	1,012	2,415
October	580	1,945
November	755	2,022
December	570	1,017
Total	7,384	24,228

Water consumption for each has been projected to 250 apartments for comparative purposes. In neither case has the hospital unit been included.

2.1 Garbage and Trash Removal

This is an area cost. In addition to location, it will vary according to the following factors:

 a. Architectural layout of trash-collecting areas.
 b. Frequency of trash collections.
 c. Central kitchen disposal provisions.
 d. Selection of trash containers and their conformity to collection methods used in the particular area.

It is also necessary to consider the special trash-problems incident to the medical unit. Many communities require ash-free incineration of infectious wastes.

2.2 Housekeeping

2.20 Housekeeping Materials and 2.21 Housekeeping Equipment

A list of materials and equipment would be cumbersome; nonetheless, the important aspects of both items cannot be underestimated. Inventory control is exceedingly crucial and, unless professionally managed, is apt to run surprisingly high. In the projects we manage we have developed forms which act as an inventory control and cross-check.

2.3 Janitor Materials

What is applicable to housekeeping is applicable to janitorial materials.

2.4 Laundry and Cleaning

First, it is necessary to decide the extent of laundry service. In other words, will the service consist of providing laundry:

 a. As needed?
 b. Daily?
 c. Weekly?
 d. Every 10 days?

Obviously, this decision, along with the number of items to be laundered, will be the basis of cost. In projects located in California, the trend is toward weekly laundry; in projects in the Pacific Northwest, every ten days. We have found weekly laundry service with a per capita linen provision of two sheets, two pillow slips, two bath towels, two face towels, two wash cloths, and one bathmat, to be adequate. (It is well to avoid personal laundry as a provision of care. Sometimes, especially in homes for the indigent elderly, it may be necessary. Such a project housing four hundred persons with, say, 25 per cent permanent bed-patients, may anticipate ten thousand pieces each week. The expense of such a service is obvious.)

Secondly, from an economic standpoint, is it best to perform the following:

a. Provide facilities and labor for a self-operated service?
b. Contract with a laundry and budget for replacements?
c. Contract with a rental service?

Some years ago it was a rule of thumb that any project housing more than twenty-five persons should operate its own laundry facility. Today, this rule is no longer applicable. Regardless of size, it is a trend to rent if possible and, if not, to contract with a laundry and budget for replacements. Let us examine the economics of such a decision by comparing costs for a facility in the Pacific Northwest, which were projected to provide weekly laundry service for 375 persons.

While in this particular instance a self-operated laundry was economically practicable, other considerations are equally important:

a. The initial cost of equipment and the cost of space relative to a self-operated service.
b. Administrative time in managing or not managing a laundry along with everything else.
c. The quality of work. If the quality of laundry is inferior, there will be dissatisfaction among the residents.
d. If contracted, the reliability of the laundry insofar as prompt delivery is concerned.
e. The standard of linen which the residence wishes to maintain.
f. Most important are the added cost of labor and the possible liabilities of another labor classification.

A. SELF-OPERATING LAUNDRY

Item	Weekly Use per Capita	Yearly Use per Capita	Weight in Lb Each	Weight per Item per Year
Sheet	2	104	1.650	171.60
Pillow slip	2	104	.350	36.40
Bath towel	2	104	.560	58.24
Face towel	2	104	.250	26.00
Wash cloth	2	104	.075	7.80
Bath mat	1	52	.660	34.32

Total per person	334.36
Total per operating ($\times$ 375 persons)	125,385.00

Description	Operating Cost per 100 Lb
Electrical	$ .026
Water	.048
Gas	.423
Supplies	.300
Labor (including fringe benefits)	6.300

Total cost per 100# volume	$7.097
Total laundry cost per year	$ 8,900
Total linen replacement	4,100
	$13,000*

*This cost does not include amortization of equipment and space.

It is necessary to realize that any laundry and cleaning estimate is inadequate if it does not include a contingency for additional requirements. This is especially true where the age profile of the residents is in the early eighties.

Since this section is concerned with resident requirements only, the costs reflected do not include dietary laundry (4.3) or hospital laundry (5.22). Nor do they include provisions for laundering maid and houseman uniforms.

2.5 Linen Replacement

The cost of linen replacement will be based upon the following:
a. Usage.
b. Quality of linen.
c. Area costs.
d. Laundry provisions.

2.6 Resident Transportation

We recently performed a survey of the leading life-care residences on the West Coast; its purpose was to substantiate parking requirement

B. CONTRACTED LAUNDRY SERVICE SCHEDULE (LAUNDRY ONLY)

Item	Weekly Use per Capita	Yearly Use per Capita	Estimate (a) Unit	Total	Estimate (b) Unit	Total	Estimate (c) Unit	Total
Laundry								
Sheet	2	104	$0.120	$12.48	$0.1000	$10.40	$0.100	$10.40
Pillow slip	2	104	0.090	9.36	0.0750	7.80	0.075	7.80
Bath towel	2	104	0.050	5.20	0.0550	5.72	0.055	5.72
Face towel	2	104	0.035	3.64	0.0325	3.38	0.040	4.16
Wash cloth	2	104	0.020	2.08	0.0325	3.38	0.020	2.08
Bath mat	1	52	0.100	5.20	0.2000	10.40	0.150	7.80
Total per person				$ 37.96		$ 41.08		$ 37.96
Total per operating (× 375 persons)				$14,200.00		$15,400.00		$14,200.00
Total linen replacement				4,100.00		4,100.00		4,100.00
				$18,300.00		$19,500.00		$18,300.00

C. CONTRACTED LAUNDRY SERVICE SCHEDULE (RENTAL SERVICE)

Item	Weekly Use per Capita	Yearly Use per Capita	Estimate (a) Unit	Total	Estimate (b) Unit	Total	Estimate (c) Unit	Total	Estimate (d) Unit	Total
Laundry										
Rental										
Sheet	2	104	$0.140	$14.56	$0.145	$15.08	$0.15	$15.60	$0.155	$16.12
Pillow slip	2	104	0.095	9.88	0.090	9.36	0.10	10.40	0.100	10.40
Bath towel	2	104	0.055	5.72	0.060	6.24	0.07	7.28	0.065	6.76
Face towel	2	104	0.040	4.16	0.040	4.16	0.05	5.20	0.050	5.20
Wash cloth	2	104	0.020	2.08	0.040	4.16	0.03	3.12	0.045	4.68
Bath mat	1	52	0.110	5.72	0.200	10.40	0.20	10.40	0.200	10.40
Total per person				$ 42.12		$ 49.40		$ 52.00		$ 53.56
Total per operating (× 375 persons)				$15,795.00		$18,525.00		$19,500.00		$20,085.00

data. It was found that 36.6 per cent of the facilities responding provided resident transportation of one type or another. There was a wide range of provisions, consisting of the following:

a. Providing trips to the doctor or hospital on an infrequent basis.
b. Providing regular trips to the doctor—usually weekly or semi-weekly.
c. Providing daily transportation.
d. Providing transportation several times daily on a predetermined schedule and route.

Obviously, infrequent provisions can best be handled by a staff member's using his own automobile on a mileage basis. (Do not forget insurance costs if this solution is used.) Somewhere between *a* and *d,* however, resident transportation is an expense sufficient to justify a budget category.

In the more elegant residences, a limousine is sometimes provided. Assuming a twenty-mile round trip four times daily, seven days a week, the limousine will travel over 29,000 miles per year. We must consider, therefore, the following:

a. The cost of labor.
b. The cost of the limousine, its maintenance, operation, and depreciation.

An added factor to the cost of labor for this twenty-mile round trip is the additional time of having to wait for residents who may be late, deviating from the established route for special purposes, and so on. If the limousine is driven 29,000 miles per year, the cost of operation could not be less than $2,900 per year ($0.10 per mile) not including labor.

Some locations are such that limousine service is imperative. Others may be located near public transportation. Sometimes it is possible to contract with a local taxicab company. Transportation will eventually become necessary, however, as the average age increases. It, of course, should be provided during inclement weather, at least. In one of our projects, which is within walking distance to shopping and one block from the bus line, we rent a limousine for periodic excursions or group trips to the theater. This cost averages about $25 per use—an economical solution if considered in the light of outright ownership.

Here we must look at the cost savings of resident transportation:

a. An excellent limousine service will encourage residents to sell their automobiles and therefore decrease the incident of accidents and any liability that might extend to the residence.

b. If fewer residents have automobiles, the necessity of expensive garage construction and maintenance is negated. (Unfortunately, many residents bring their automobiles originally and then sell them; this frequently results in a garage or parking facility which is only *partially* used but which must be *fully* amortized.)

c. An excellent limousine service will have social benefits since nondriving residents will not be confined to activities within the project. If outside interests are not encouraged, the residence will rapidly become concentric.

d. If the garage is such that only an attendant can park autos, a limousine service is an economical solution in itself.

2.7 Window Cleaning

The cost of window cleaning depends entirely upon the design and location of the building. A single-story, campus-style project in central California will be able to handle window cleaning as a part of general maintenance; a facility (without balconies) in the Pacific Northwest, housing three hundred persons, may spend $5,400 annually. Clearly, then, the budget item for window washing depends upon these factors:

a. Design and building type.

b. Location and climatic conditions.

In any event, it is wise to budget for supplemental maintenance costs, even if the design and location admit of window washing as a standard maintenance item.

2.8 Operating Payroll

Operating payroll is one of our most important costs. It includes the costs of the following labor classifications, each of which will be discussed separately:

a. Telephone operator.

b. Executive housekeeper.

c. Maid.

d. Houseman.

Telephone Operator

This cost depends upon the type of telephone system selected, as outlined under 2.08. If, for example, a PBX system is used in an operation consisting of 250 apartments, it is well to budget for two full-time operators and two part-time operators, each working two eight-hour days. Should the system, however, preclude switching the lines into the nurses' station during the midnight-to-morning shift or allowing the watchman or some other person to operate the switchboard during this shift, an additional full-time operator plus her weekend replacement must be added to the budget. Some projects discontinue switchboard service from midnight till morning. We strongly recommend that this practice, though economically attractive, be avoided.

Executive Housekeeper

The similarities between life-care housing for our elders and hotel techniques are obvious throughout this work. The executive housekeeper is no less important to life-care housing than to first-rate hotel administration. In many ways, she is more important. The nontransitory characteristics of a life-care residence as well as the demands of an elderly population are taxing upon the most adept housekeeping operation. An excellent example is provided by time and motion studies. Vast differentials occur, based upon demands of the residents. Some are justifiable; others are not. If the added service is necessary physically or mentally, or even sociologically, it is probably acceptable. Often, however, a resident will look upon a maid as her personal maid and demand services beyond the limits of the project budget. This, of course, sometimes presents problems for the administrator. It is imperative that the housekeeping operation be organized to maximum effectiveness at the outset of the operation. On our projects we usually employ the executive housekeeper at least one month prior to opening. During this time, she organizes the entire housekeeping schedule. The maids and houseman report to her directly.

Maid

The number of maids is determined by the extent of housekeeping services. The extent of housekeeping services depends upon the following:

(1) Whether or not the maids clean the residents' apartments.

(2) If they clean the residents' apartments, How often? Daily? Weekly? Every ten days? Every two weeks?

(3) In cleaning the residents' apartments, do they also change the bed linen? Do they change the bed linen each time they clean the apartment? Or do they simply leave clean linens for the residents to change? Some administrators feel that it is psychologically beneficial for the female residents to change their own bed linens; they feel that this eases the transfer or disengagement from an independent to a life-care living experience. This is not as significant a savings as it appears since, in any event, the maids will clean the bathroom, which is most time-consuming. The median average length of time required to clean a studio apartment is only five minutes less than that required to clean a one-bedroom apartment. An additional labor cost is the time required to defrost and clean refrigerator units if they are provided as a part of the kitchenette. This could be alleviated by units which are frostfree and installed at an accessible level.

(4) The number of maids will depend also on the type of project. For the reasons stated above, it takes less time to clean a two-room apartment (apart from the linen service) than two studio apartments. Since the number of maids is also based upon the number of rooms that a maid can clean in one day, there is, once again, a relationship of design to cost. (See Project Summary in Appendix.)

Let us assume that maid service will consist of heavy housekeeping weekly, which includes changing bed and bath linens. Let us also assume a normal apartment composition ranging from studios to two-bedroom, two-bath units, and typical life-care non-apartment areas: under these circumstances, a maid can clean from twelve to fifteen rooms per day (a bathroom is considered a room).

Houseman

To an extent, what has been said about the maids is applicable to the houseman. Assuming the same conditions for our example as those mentioned above, a residence of 250 apartments will require 3.5 housemen.

CATEGORY 3—MAINTENANCE COSTS

3.0 Contract Services		$_____
3.01 Elevators	$_____	
3.02 Exterminators	_____	
3.03 Patrol Service	_____	
3.04 Watchman Service	_____	
3.05 Miscellaneous Appliances (Repairs)	_____	
3.1 Decorating		_____
3.2 Furniture and Furnishings		_____
3.20 Carpets	_____	
3.21 Draperies	_____	
3.22 Furniture	_____	
3.3 Ground Materials and Equipment		_____
3.4 Insurance		
3.41 Fire	_____	
3.42 Furniture and Furnishings	_____	
3.43 Liability	_____	
3.44 Property	_____	
3.45 Other	_____	
3.5 Repairs and General Maintenance		_____
3.6 Vehicles		_____
3.60 Interest and Amortization	_____	
3.61 Maintenance	_____	
3.62 Repairs	_____	
3.63 Rentals	_____	
3.7 Unassigned		_____
3.8 Maintenance Payroll		_____
3.9 Other		_____
Total Maintenance		$_____

3.0 Contract Services

3.01 Elevators

Three alternatives are possible:

    a. Self-maintenance.

    b. Parts, oil, and grease (p.o.g.) maintenance.

    c. Full maintenance.

While the maintenance costs on a p.o.g. basis may appear economical, we must consider the consequences of anything other than full maintenance. In many of the projects we have studied, residents disliked elevators. In one project, one of the residents always made it a practice to loiter around the elevator lobby so she wouldn't have to ride the elevator alone. In another project, an eighty-year-old woman preferred climbing two flights of stairs to riding on the elevator. Several such instances illustrate the necessity of a flawless elevator operation. Admittedly, from a cost standpoint, a p.o.g. contract is about two thirds that of a full maintenance contract; the liabilities, however, outweigh any savings.

3.02 Exterminators

This is a minimal cost and is basically an area cost. It is almost negligible for a high-rise reinforced-concrete or steel-frame building. In some instances a ground preparation may be necessary prior to construction to alleviate higher exterminating costs.

3.03 Patrol Service

Patrol service is simply an arrangement with the local police to give special consideration to the retirement residence. This service should supplement the watchman service.

3.04 Watchman Service

The watchman service in a home for our elders consists of more than appears obvious. First, we must consider the basic security need of elderly persons. Many of our residents became interested in life-care projects because of a fear for person and property in their existing living environment. Sometimes this reason is unspoken. Usually it is implied. It is important to the residents, therefore, that a watchman, armed and uniformed, be on duty from midnight till morning, at least. The watchman is sometimes used to operate the switchboard between rounds. (While on his rounds the switchboard control is transferred to the nurses' station.)

In most projects one watchman with weekend relief is sufficient. In a new structure, especially one with a garage building, his work may be aided by electronic devices. A typical example is an electric-eye connection attached to the residents' automobiles so that they alone have unconditional ingress and egress from the building. Here a decision must be made as to the advantages of a contracted or noncontracted service. A contracted service has the advantage of a service professionally handled with a reputation that, in itself, adds security to the building. A contracted service generally provides a watchman (seven nights per week) who is uniformed, armed, and bonded. The charge is a flat hourly rate. Many projects have selected a contracted service because of the unavailability of really qualified watchmen. We have seen examples of both contracted and self-operated services which were satisfactory. Basically, the decision rests on the availability of personnel. Needless to say, a self-operated watchman service is less expensive. It becomes simply a matter of weighing these savings against the assets of a professional service.

3:05 *Miscellaneous Appliances (Repairs)*

This term is self-descriptive and refers of course to management-owned appliances. We generally budget $4,500 for a 250-unit project.

3.1 Decorating

In certain states the law requires that an apartment be repainted after each vacancy. This is an excellent practice in housing for our elders whether or not it is required under law. The tenancy change in a retirement residence is based upon so many factors that it is impossible to estimate it within the confines of this section. Under state laws which require mandatory reserves, it is better to include this sum in the overall reserves which are required by statute.

3.2 Furniture and Furnishings

This item should also be reflected in the overall reserves in certain jurisdictions. Furniture and furnishings may be very cheap or very expensive. They may have a short or long life-span. Consequently, the budget amount for this item admits of wide variations. In some projects, furniture for the residents' apartments as well as for the common areas is provided. This may be necessary in housing for the

indigent aged; it is not necessary, however, in housing for the middle-
and upper-income elderly. Generally, it is inadvisable.

Most persons prefer to bring their own furniture and furnishings.
In this way they are able to lessen the trauma which sometimes accom-
panies moving into housing specifically intended for elderly persons.
Usually, the only furniture and furnishings provided by management
are the following:

a. Carpets and draperies in all areas including residents' apartments.
b. Furniture and furnishings for the common areas.
c. Furniture and furnishings for the medical unit as described
   under 5.20.

Nonetheless, the cost of furniture required is considerable. The
lounge furniture for one of our projects consisted of sixty-three items
at a cost in excess of $6,000. Still, the lounge on this project repre-
sents but 9 per cent of the total public space not including the
medical center. The life span of furniture in life-care housing will
vary from five to ten years. It is necessary that management be
cautious in selecting furniture that will conform to the life span
upon which the budget is based. The cost of furniture and furnishings will vary, again, according to the amount of space to be furnished: Will there be maximal or minimal common areas? How
much floor area is to be carpeted? For how many windows will
draperies be provided? What type of rods will be used? What type of
carpet: Wool? Nylon? Acrilan®? Each has its advantages and disadvantages. Wool carpeting has stain problems while nylon is non-
absorbent. Acrilan has some of the advantages of both; it also has some
of the disadvantages. It will be necessary to use different types of
carpeting for different areas. Some types of carpeting are static-free;
this is a particularly important consideration in dry climates. Similarly,
it will be necessary to select drapery material which will conform to
the fire prevention laws in certain states.

3.3 Ground Materials and Equipment

This cost will depend upon the amount of landscaping and ground
area to be maintained. It will range from a negligible amount in an

urban project to a significant amount in a project located on, say, forty or fifty acres.

3.4 Insurance

3.41 Fire

Fire insurance is based upon the area in which the project is located as well as the type of structure. Here, the consultant must work with the architect to assure design characteristics that will be conducive to attractive rates.

3.42 Furniture and Furnishings, 3.43 Liability, and 3.44 Property

Each of these categories of insurance is self-explanatory.

3.45 Other

On our projects we recommend extra-expense insurance to cover the additional expense of having to house residents elsewhere while a section of the apartment building is being repaired because of fire or some other cause. Its cost is negligible. In certain areas earthquake insurance may be advisable. Its cost, we might mention, is exorbitant.

3.5 Repairs and General Maintenance

This item refers to a cost other than replacement reserves described under Category 6. It provides for multitudinous minor item repairs as well as general maintenance. In states with statutory reserve requirements it may be wise to include this item in the overall reserves.

3.6 Vehicles

In certain projects it may become necessary to own or rent vehicles other than those considered under items 1.7 and 2.6. If, for example, a project must maintain fifty acres of landscaping, the necessity of owning pickup trucks, power mowers, fertilizers, and so on, is apparent. A project of six acres, on the other hand, may find extensive equipment ownership unfeasible. It will probably be less expensive to rent equipment as needed. This decision is, of course, based upon the projected operating criteria. If owning one or more vehicles is necessary, the costs of interest and amortization, maintenance, and repairs should be reflected in the budget. If vehicle rental is satisfactory, the cost will depend upon rental rates in the particular area.

3.8 Maintenance Payroll*

Many of the considerations applicable to the housekeeping payroll will apply to the maintenance payroll. The principal classifications are as follows:

    a. Superintendent of maintenance.
    b. Maintenance man.
    c. Gardener.
    d. Watchman (if not contracted).†

Superintendent of Maintenance

This classification is generally adequate where there are no high-pressure boilers and a bona fide building-engineer is not required. (Needless to say, a building engineer is a higher-salaried employee.) The superintendent of maintenance has the responsibility for the operation of all facilities as well as the electrical and mechanical equipment necessary for the following:

    (1) Ventilation.
    (2) Production of steam and hot water.
    (3) Water for washing and consumption.
    (4) Refrigeration.
    (5) Steam for laundry and kitchen.
    (6) Lighting.
    (7) Communication.

He also has the responsibility of the maintenance of the building and all of its equipment. In addition to the maintenance personnel under his direction, he has the responsibility of all crafts which may be employed occasionally for various types of repair work.

Since the uninterrupted mechanical functioning of the project is

---

*Item 3.7 is unassigned.
†Discussed under item 3.04.

his responsibility, it is well to budget on the high side for the wage of such a person. The wage scale range will depend, of course, upon the rates prevalent in a particular area. We have found it to be good practice to employ the superintendent of maintenance as a mechanical and electrical inspector during the later construction phase, thereby greatly simplifying the transition period from construction to operation.

Maintenance Man

The number of maintenance personnel required will depend upon the following factors:

(1) The size of the project.
(2) The type of project (campus or high-rise).
(3) Extent of common areas to be maintained.
(4) Extent of medical facilities.

In the light of the above-mentioned factors, three maintenance men will be adequate for most 250-apartment projects.

Gardener

The number of gardeners will depend upon the area of the project. While 1.5 gardeners may be adequate for a six-acre site with land-scaping which is reasonably easy to maintain, as many as seven gardeners may be necessary for a thirty-acre site with awkward landscaping. At one time it was a rule of thumb that landscaping should be limited to an area maintainable by one gardener. The attraction of high-priced facilities has, however, rendered this rule obsolete. This, incidentally, is another decision which must be considered in the selection of a site. Sometimes it is wise to use a contracted gardening service, particularly in facilities with minimal ground areas.

Another item which may be quite expensive is exterior repainting for a frame-stucco building; the same cost will be negligible on a high-rise building where exterior repainting is usually limited to handrails and a minimum amount of trim. The former is so absolutely dependent upon construction costs and area conditions that it is impossible to consider it in a general sense; the latter should not exceed $1,000 per year in a high-rise building of less than 250 apartments.

CATEGORY 4—DIETARY COSTS*

4.0 Self-operated or Contracted Food-service		$....................
4.1 Employee Meals		....
4.10 Administrative	$....................	
4.11 Operational	....	
4.12 Maintenance	....	
4.13 Dietary	....	
4.14 Medical	....	
4.2 Raw-food Cost		....
4.3 Laundry and Linen		....
4.4 Linen Replacement		....
4.5 Supplies		....
4.6 Unassigned		....
4.7 Unassigned		....
4.8 Dietary Payroll		....
4.9 Other		....
Total Dietary		$....................

4.0 Self-operated or Contracted Food-service

The trend in contemporary homes for the elderly is to contract the food service. Sometimes the size, location, or type of residence prohibits a contracted service. A home with twenty persons, for example, would offer no inducement for a food contractor. A home with ninety or one hundred persons may be large enough to consider a food contract. A home with food costs in excess of $100,000 should definitely consider a food contractor.

Let us consider the disadvantages of a food contract:

   a. The control of this most important item is in the hands of an outside firm.

   b. The food contractor is making a profit which could be used to upgrade the quality or quantity of food or the efficiency of service.

   c. The advantages of professional management may be realized by an administrator with extensive hotel-restaurant experience.

Now let us consider the advantages:

   a. While the control of this item is in the hands of an outside

---

*Many excellent books are available on the techniques of restaurant operations. The purpose of this section is simply to embellish such knowledge with a description of the problems peculiar to housing for our elders.

firm, it is a rare administrator who is able to equal the professional standards of food specialists.

b. Generally, any profit the food contractor might make will be offset by operational efficiency, buying power, and the alleviation of many administrative headaches.

c. A food contractor generally has a positive psychological effect upon the happiness of the residents. They know that the food service is in professional hands.

d. Under a fixed-fee contract, the contractor maintains the dishware inventory. This will run in the neighborhood of $5,000 per year for two hundred residents. This convenience is a part of the management cost.

Decisions Affecting the Economics and Quality of Service

Whether the home decides to operate its own dining room or contract the food service, certain decisions must be made:

BUDGET

The most important decision is, of course, the amount the home can afford to spend for the operation of its dining room. On the West Coast these costs range from $51 to $150 per resident per month. (An aside: cost and quality do not always follow. We have seen instances of homes with $60 budgets pleasing their residents as opposed to homes with $120 budgets subject to constant complaint.)

NUMBER OF MEALS

The second most important decision is the number of meals to be served each day. Obviously, the cost of serving two meals will be less than three; or one meal less than two. But this is not in direct proportion. For example, the cost of kitchen equipment, depreciation, and so on remains constant; the cost of the head chef and most kitchen personnel also remains constant. In some areas it is difficult to get any but full-time employees, which means that the labor costs for one or two meals is just about the same. Also, where fewer than three meals are served, the residents tend to gorge themselves.

STYLE OF SERVICE

The style of service is next in importance. Obviously, cafeteria or buffet style is cheapest. While it may be pleasant, it often is impractical in a home for the elderly. This is due to the inability of many residents to manipulate trays. Also, in some states cafeteria service is prohibited under law.

Sometimes a family style is a pleasant solution. The food is placed in the center of the table and everyone helps himself. This will, of course, reduce the number of waitresses and waiters required. (The kitchen staff, however, remains the same.) The most successful solution (and the solution sometimes required by law) is table service at all meals with the possible exception of a buffet breakfast and, perhaps, a Sunday-night buffet.

NUMBER OF MENU SELECTIONS

The number of menu selections is next in importance. The greater the scope of selections, the greater the costs. The addition of a third entrée onto a two-entrée menu is likely to increase costs from $12 to $20 per person per month. The cost is not in raw food. A wise food manager can buy food for a multi-entrée menu and end up with few leftovers. The cost is in labor: the cost of a waitress' time while the residents make up their minds. This basic problem is compounded many times when there is a choice of vegetable, starch, dessert, salad, and so on.

SPECIAL DIETS

Next, we must consider the number and scope of special diets. One residence we have studied has reached an almost impossible impasse due to nearly all of its residents' being on special diets. Most of them are self-imposed. Special diets, if handled correctly, should present no problems. It is recommended that special diets be subject to medical authorization.

Some facilities require persons restricted to special diets to sit in a special dining room. This, we think, is unnecessarily oppressive. Others require them to come to dinner a few minutes earlier to allow the kitchen to prepare special diets. Most facilities are able to manage special diets during the course of the meal period.

SEATING CAPACITY OF DINING ROOM

The size of the dining room is important. An undersized dining room with residents choosing an early or late meal hour is economically sound in that it reduces the number of employees who are, for the most part, working eight hours. The disadvantage is in a sense of undue regimentation if residents are scheduled to certain meal hours or constant aggravation if they are forced to wait.

LENGTH OF MEAL PERIOD

The length of the meal period will alter costs. A long meal period will cause delays in cleaning up and problems in table service. Generally, while it increases cost it adds greatly to resident satisfaction.

LABOR CLASSIFICATIONS

Whether or not the residence is under union jurisdiction will affect costs not only in labor rates and fringe benefits but in the degree of job classification. For example: Can the waitresses help in the kitchen or must their work be confined to serving tables? Is there a chief cook with subordinate cooks, or is there a chief cook with cook 2, cook 3, and cook 4—all with different wage classifications (item 4.8)?

LINEN OR PAPER PLACE-SETTINGS

Will linen or paper place-settings be used? In the early homes a continuous table cloth with the chronicle of the week's menu was standard practice. The trend is to use linen at dinner and paper place-settings at lunch and breakfast. The cost of laundry and linen replacement or the cost of linen rental are decisions that are best made on an area basis. Naturally, a high-quality linen will increase costs. Normally, linen will increase the operating cost in the neighborhood of around two dollars per resident per month even if it is used for dinner only.

UNIFORMS

The uniforms for food personnel may present a cost factor. Usually, if the uniform is other than a plain black or white uniform, the cost is carried by the employer. In some states this practice is set by precedent, in others by law. It will generally increase the cost $1,400 per year. This is assuming a normal life span of the uniforms.

EMPLOYEE MEALS

Historically, all dietary employees are given at least one meal during the period they work. Whether or not the remaining employees are given meals is a management or, in some instances, a labor contract decision (item 4.1).

AFTERNOON TEA OR BEDTIME SNACK

An interesting addition to the dietary budget is the serving of afternoon tea or a bedtime snack. A residence of three hundred persons, for example, will spend between $900 and $1,500 per month for an afternoon tea service.

TRAY SERVICE

Early in the course of operation, it is necessary to arrive at a policy decision regarding tray service to residents' apartments. Sometimes it will be economical to provide tray service if a resident is too sick to come to meals but not sick enough to require bed care. Trays not authorized by the staff physician, however, can become a costly item. In a campus-style residence for over 250 persons (without a hospital), 1,100 trays were delivered during one of the winter months. This averages out to thirty-nine trays per day. If it took an average of ten minutes to deliver each tray, this would require 11,700 minutes or 195 hours per month. At $1.60 per hour, this would cost $312 per month. It may be wise, therefore, to make a slight charge, at least for trays not authorized by the staff physician.

DISHWARE

The quality of dishware is another important consideration. Here it is necessary to compromise between pleasant appearance and lasting qualities of dishware. In buying the initial inventory, both aspects must be considered. It may be possible also to buy more than one pattern to help relieve the monotony of the service. The replacement cost of $5,000 (mentioned under 4.0, advantage *d*) permits an extremely durable quality of dishware.

Some Problems of Operation

We have considered most of these items from a budget standpoint. Now we must examine the problem in greater depth.

Residents in a home for the elderly will be eating three meals a day in the same dining room for a number of years. It is bound to become monotonous. Unless management is perpetually alert, it is likely to become stereotyped. A resident who lives at a home for fifteen years and eats three meals a day in the dining room will eat over 16,400 consecutive meals in the same atmosphere. If any of us ate 16,400 meals at our favorite restaurant it would eventually become tiring. Even if a resident eats out once a week, it still totals 15,600 meals. There are many ways to avoid the monotony inherent to this situation:

    a. A continental or buffet breakfast served in different areas to smaller groups. This can be done with a minimum labor force and allows an extended meal period without seriously affecting the budget.

    b. Variations in dishware design.

    c. Frequently redecorating the dining room. (This, of course, is an extremely expensive solution.)

    d. Occasional barbecues, cookouts, special dinners for the Fourth of July, and so on.

    e. A Sunday-afternoon buffet.

    f. Another solution (usually unplanned) is that of a continual upgrading of quality and selection to the point of a first-rate service. Usually the reverse happens. A project starts out with a prohibitively high budget figure and spends every dollar; then management decides to cut back and obvious problems occur. It is wisest to start with a more conservative menu and then upgrade the service. During the planning stages of a project, an inferior food service may appear attractive from a cost standpoint. Needless to say, actual experience with going operations indicates the futility of such a decision.

The type of personnel used in the dining room also has an enormous effect upon the success of the food service. At one home in Oregon, all the waiters and waitresses are high school and college students. The residents seem to tolerate what at times appears to be inept service because the young persons remind them of their grandchildren. Sometimes the attitude of staff will make all the difference between an enjoyable and a tolerable meal. Selecting the staff presents greater than normal restaurant problems because of the following:

a. Waiting on elderly persons may be difficult and depressing for some employees.
b. There are no tips. It is possible to make more money from tips by working in a commercial restaurant. (Usually, this is partially overcome by allowing the residents to contribute to a Christmas bonus fund.)

If it has been decided that the dietary department will be managed by a food contractor, two contract types are possible: fixed fee contract and management contract.

If a fixed fee is used, the following (in addition to food, labor, and management) may be included:

a. Laundry and linen.
b. Liability insurance.
c. Maintenance of inventory.
d. Maintenance of kitchen.
e. Maintenance of dining room.
f. Uniforms.
g. Utilities.

A fixed fee has a distinct and obvious advantage from a budget standpoint in that it guarantees cost. On the other hand, it has disadvantages if a really accurate cost accounting is not maintained for the residence. Food costs are sensitive; as a consequence, the contractor may be inclined to take his profit off the top and cut back on quality and quantity. This, we must admit, is a negligible criticism since most contracts can be rewritten to increase costs to the advantage of both parties.

A management contract allows direct control of expenditures for food and labor. Generally, it consists of cost plus a fixed management fee. (Sometimes, however, the management fee is calculated on a resident-meal basis.) Under a management contract, all employees (with the exception of the food manager) are paid directly by the residence. All food costs are billed directly to the residence. The management contractor is selling efficiency of operation and the privilege of using his buying power.

4.1 Employee Meals

While dietary employees, as previously noted, have historically received those meals which occur during their work day, it is a management decision as to whether or not nondietary employees are to receive meals. Generally, it is limited to one meal per day, and the decision is based upon the location of the residence (that is, distance to restaurants) and the practice of the area. In some instances, meals are given as a fringe benefit; in others, the employee pays for each meal on an individual basis. Assuming that this cost equals $.50 per employee (minimum) and assuming that the administrator, executive housekeeper, superintendent of maintenance, nursing-department head, and all dietary employees receive one meal per day under the contract, the additional cost of employee meals (one meal only) for a residence housing 340 persons, with a fifty-bed medical center, would be as follows:

4.10 Administration employees	$ 500
4.11 Operational employees	2,100
4.12 Maintenance employees	600
4.14 Medical employees	2,900
	$6,100

4.2 Raw-food Cost

Raw-food cost will equal between 35 per cent and 51 per cent of the entire dietary operating budget. A discussion of buying practices would be cumbersome. It is, however, important to emphasize that raw food is such an expensive item that costs must be reevaluated continuously. Only an inept administrator allows his food manager to act with complete independence, even under a contracted food service.

Recent trends toward frozen food have presented interesting problems. Many kitchens have been rendered obsolete by inadequate frozen-food storage areas. Also, prepackaged frozen food, while difficult (but not impossible) to examine in the light of competitive bidding, offers attractions insofar as consistency of quality is concerned.

4.3 Laundry and Linen and 4.4 Linen Replacement

Laundry and linen costs will be based upon the size of the items and the frequency of use. The importance of this cost should not be understated. Let us assume that linen is used at the evening meal, and paper place-settings and napkins at breakfast and lunch. In a residence with three hundred residents in an area where napkins are laundered for one cent each, this cost will be as follows:

$$300 \times 365 \times .01 = \$1,095 \text{ or} \qquad \$1,100$$

and tablecloths 72″ square are laundered for .10 each:

$$300 \div 4 \text{ (table seating 4)} \times 365$$
$$\times .10 = \$2,737 \text{ or} \qquad 2,700$$

and dish cloths   200
                                                       ——————
                                                        $4,000
Linen replacement should equal   2,500
                                                       ——————
                                                        $6,500

In addition, paper place-settings for the remaining
meals should equal   2,200
                                                       ——————
                            Total $8,700

4.5 Supplies

The cost of supplies, including paper place-settings, uniforms and so forth, should vary between 5 per cent and 11 per cent of the dietary costs.

4.8 Dietary Payroll*

This item will equal from 42 per cent to 49 per cent of the dietary department budget, depending upon the factors discussed in the early part of this section. While job classifications will vary from area to area, classification under a union jurisdiction will be the most carefully defined. In certain jurisdictions they include the following:

a. Head cook.
b. Second cook.
c. Third cook.
d. All other cooks.
e. Pastry cook.
f. Baker.
g. Head waitress (sometimes hostess).

*4.6 and 4.7 are unassigned.

h. Waitress and waiter.

i. Head dishwasher.

j. Dishwashers and potwashers.

k. Vegetable man.

l. Salad girl.

m. Kitchen helper.

CATEGORY 5—MEDICAL

The Objective

The most important part of life-care is medical care. It would seem, therefore, that its eventual aim would be to encompass, without deductibles or time limitations,* "total medical care." While the phrase "total care" is often used, it is seldom practiced. Generally, however, *nearly* total medical care is possible within practicable economic limits, that is, total medical care except for certain exclusions. These exclusions follow a typical pattern: ophthalmology beyond the provisions of Medicare,† chiropody, chiropractic, dentistry, mechanical aids, religious sect, and preexisting illness.‡

Medicare

At the outset it is well to describe the fundamentals of Medicare and how they relate to the medical phase of the life-care program which we have described.

---

*The argument of commercial insurance carriers is brought to mind, namely, that deductibles tend to discourage malingerers, hypochondriacs, and so on. Unfortunately, deductibles also discourage preventive medicine due to the typical elderly person's delay in investigating early symptoms. Most important, the nature of geriatic medicine is out of context with most commercial insurance interpretations.

†Ophthalmology is sometimes given under a clinic contract, but management usually has the right to terminate it if it becomes excessively burdensome. A significant percentage of hospitalized residents are hospitalized for ophthalmologic treatment. Ophthalmological problems will eventually be included since Medicare substantially reduces this risk factor.

‡Preexisting illness is a nebulous phrase. It usually refers to an existing disease or to a disease which has a recurrence sufficiently imminent to unbalance the economic averages. During one of our early studies, I recall asking a Catholic Sister who had been the administrator of a home for the aged for many years, "What percentage of your residents has a heart condition?" She replied, "They all have a heart condition, it's part of being old." In short, preexisting illness does not exclude conditions natural to old age.

A. Hospital Care

Medicare provides sixty days of hospital care in a general hospital with a $40 deductible; it provides an additional thirty days for the patient (or, in this case, the facility) paying a small portion of the cost per day. Subject to the patient's having been in the hospital three days or longer, there is an additional benefit of twenty days at no cost and eighty days with a slight cost for hospitalization in an extended care facility.§

Medicare hospitalization may be likened to an inverted equilateral triangle. The base represents hospital care which gradually phases into extended care. It is important to remember that the philosophy of Medicare is towards alleviating the excruciating need of hospital care among our elderly population. Extended care, again, is only a phase-out benefit. Hospital care is related to a spell-of-illness factor which is defined quite simply, namely: Any time a patient has been out of a hospital for sixty days or longer his next hospital visit, if it is for the same disease or treatment, will commence a new term of illness. This, like the remaining Medicare statements, is an oversimplification; it would be impossible to define Medicare in detail in this work. Utilization review committees, licensing standards, accounting principles, and so on are enormously complex. Excellent materials are available from the Department of Public Health and the Social Security Administration.

B. Physician's Care

Under physician's care the patient (or facility) pays the first $50 per year of physician's cost and 20 per cent of the physician's cost thereafter. Medicare pays for the remainder subject to the physician's cost's being acceptable to the fees established as reasonable by the Federal Government.

---

§Extended-care facility is a new definition of hospital type. It is less than a general or specialized hospital but more than a long-term-care facility (sometimes referred to as a convalescent hospital or nursing home). There has been a "fall-out" benefit to society by forcing the latter to upgrade standards or remain disqualified for Medicare benefits. For the purposes of this work the terms chronic care facility, convalescent hospital, or nursing home may be used synonymously for long-term-care facility. The phrase extended-care facility, however, will be used only for that specific kind of facility.

C. Outpatient Diagnostic Coverage

Under outpatient diagnostic coverage the patient (or facility) pays the first $20 and 20 per cent of the remaining costs for each diagnostic service furnished by the same hospital for a twenty-day period. This service is infrequently used since a good part of it can be supplied by the facility on the premises. Other parts can be supplied by the laboratory and x-ray facilities available at the clinic or at the office of the physician used by the facility.

D. Home Care

This benefit relates to care provided in the resident's apartment. It allows a more refined gradation of care from hospital to home than was previously possible. Under Part A of Medicare, a patient is allowed one hundred visits per year at no cost; under Part B of Medicare, he is allowed one hundred visits at 20 per cent of the cost, less $50 deductible. (This is the same deductible described under B above; there are not two deductibles.) Home care is usually provided by a visiting-nurses' association. A visiting-nurses' association, in addition to the services of a registered nurse, generally provides at least one of the five following specialties: (1) physical therapy; (2) occupational therapy; (3) speech therapy; (4) social work; (5) health services (assistance with bathing, and so forth).

E. Miscellaneous Considerations

There are certain considerations which must be examined minutely in order to accurately estimate costs in the light of Medicare. Eyeglasses and eye examinations for the purpose of prescribing, fitting, or changing eyeglasses are not covered by most facilities or by Medicare. Routine physical examinations are not covered by Medicare, but any good facility provides them as a regular part of the medical program. Medicare pays for in-hospital drugs. Here management must decide whether or not the facility intends to pay for out-of-hospital drugs. Neither Medicare nor most facilities pay for routine dentistry. (At present Medicare pays for dentistry associated with surgery resulting from illness or accident.) It should be mentioned, however, that the consulting services of a dentist should be interrelated with a good extended-care facility. Neither Medicare nor most facilities pay for hearing aids or examinations for hearing aids. Medicare does not pay for immunizations. Most facilities provide some immunizations such as flu shots, as determined necessary by the staff physician. Neither Medicare nor most facilities pay for vaccinations required for traveling abroad. Medicare pays for 50 per cent of the reasonable charges for outside hospitalization treatment for mental, psychoneurotic, and personality disorders up to a limit of $250 per year. A good life-care facility might exclude treatment by a psychiatrist but will cover mental hospitalization without limit; under Medicare there is a lifetime limit of 190 days. Neither Medicare nor most life-care facilities cover the services of a chiropractor, osteopath, chiropodist, or religious practitioner.

Again, while incomplete, this section is sufficient to delineate some cost items affected by Medicare. Still, a word of caution: Medicare is limited to persons sixty-five years of age or older (there may be a few persons under sixty-five at a life-care residence), and some persons have not registered for the supplemental coverage under Part B of Medicare. It is recommended that those planning homes for our elders interrelate their goals not only with Medicare but with supplementary state-programs.

5.0	Outpatient Reserve Fund		$_____
5.1	Physician Service Contract		_____
5.2	Medical Center (Long-term-care Unit) Operation		_____
	5.20 Furniture	$_____	
	5.21 Supplies	_____	
	5.22 Laundry and Cleaning	_____	
	5.23 Linen Replacement	_____	
5.3	Insurance		_____
	5.30 Hospital	_____	
	5.31 Nursing Home	_____	
	5.32 Surgical	_____	
	5.33 Physician	_____	
	5.34 Bed Reservation	_____	
5.4	Malpractice Insurance		_____
5.5	Stop-loss Policy		_____
5.6	Unassigned		_____
5.7	Unassigned		_____
5.8	Medical Payroll		_____
5.9	Other		_____
	Total Medical		$_____

5.0 Outpatient Reserve Fund (or Hospitalization Fund)

The soundest approach is to budget for outside hospitalization.

The amount is usually calculated on a per capita basis and will vary according to the scope of care and the extent of hospitalization which must be provided off the premises.

It is typical of a life-care residence that for the most part the early hospitalization costs are for acute care. This is due to the fact that the age group is younger, and the incident of disease correctable by surgery is greater; and the fact that many persons postpone unimportant surgical procedures until they move into the residence.*

As the project increases in age, the majority of diseases requiring bed care will be chronic illnesses which require extensive, long-term hospitalization. This type of care does not, for the most part, come under Medicare since it must be remembered that care in an extended-care facility is essentially "postgeneral hospital care." This care is true long-term care.

It is not uncommon for a new residence to have an experience factor of two acute hospital-days per resident; nor is it uncommon for a fifteen-year-old residence to lower this to one-half hospital-days per resident. The inverse ratio of chronic-care days is, of course, even more disproportionate. It is ideal if chronic care can be provided on the premises and given under the same auspices as that of the life-care residence. While early requirements may be met with a small bed-capacity (say 10 per cent of the residents), the eventual requirements in twelve to fifteen years will be 17 per cent and then, in a few years, will level out at 20 per cent.

During the early development stage of any project with a large medical facility, a decision must be made as to how much chronic care is to be made available to outside patients (that is, nonresidents). The dilemma stems from supporting a large facility during the early and economically difficult years of operation. Subject to tax problems and subject to the health profile of the residence, it is sometimes feasible to set aside beds in excess of 10 per cent of the resident population for outside patients. Here, however, management must choose the patients and estimate their length of stay with extreme caution.

---

*Costs resulting from this latter reason can be lessened by physical examinations conducted just prior to occupancy. In some states such examinations are required under law.

Bed Reservation*

It sometimes happens that a residence for the elderly will have provided an insufficient number of chronic-care beds (or no beds at all) and be located in an area where there is a shortage of long-term care facilities. In this case it may be necessary to reserve beds at a nearby convalescent hospital. A stipulated amount per expected bed usage may be paid the hospital for the privilege of having beds available when they are needed. In most cases, however, the opposite is true; that is, convalescent hospitals are so anxious to provide beds for retirement residence patients that they offer a reduced rate per month per patient or a flat rate irrespective of the degree of care required. In an area where the average cost is, say, $550 per patient per month, the convalescent hospital may offer care for $475 per month, realizing that there will be a variation in care required, but that, in the long run, it will average $475.

5.1 Physician Service Contract

Three basic approaches to medical care are available under a life-care program:

    a. Policy with commercial carrier.

    b. Contract with a physician or group of physicians for daily visits to the premises, and budget for any physicians' service beyond this routine.

    c. Contracting with a clinic.

Policy with Commercial Carrier

This would be a policy for both physicians' services and hospitalization. Since hospitalization, as applied to life-care programs, has been discussed earlier, these evaluations will concentrate on physicians' services. Such a policy is similar to any group policy except that to approach total care, the gaps of coverage must be taken into account and considered in the operating budget, that is, deductibles, and the corridor between the group policy, Medicare, and major medical. The advantages and disadvantages are as follows:

---

*Since this item (though a form of insurance) relates to hospital problems, it is discussed here rather than under Item 5.34 as listed in the *pro forma*.

ADVANTAGES

(1) Burden of possible excessive losses carried by commercial carrier.

(2) Security in knowing insurance is carried by a well-established insurance firm. (This may have particular advantages during the sales of the units.)

(3) Availability of insurance while away from the immediate area of the facility.

DISADVANTAGES

(1) Complexity of budget for deductibles and corridors if a plan approaching total care is envisioned.

(2) Illogical circumstance of a life-care program carrying a policy which in all probability will have a cancellation clause.

(3) At the time expenses are low, almost every available medical budget dollar is being spent to pay premiums. This permits the danger of cancellation by the carrier at the time medical expenses are highest. At such a time the chances are that the facility will be without a reserve medical budget due to the initial expense of the premium. In fact, it could bring about the nearly insurmountable problem of commencing the medical program on a different basis, that is, with an average age of, say, eighty-three instead of seventy-four.

Contract with Physicians for Residential Visits and Budget for Additional Service

This approach may be on the basis of a fixed fee, say, $600 per month for routine clinic, or on a per-resident treatment basis. The advantages and disadvantages are as follows:

ADVANTAGES

(1) The facility would be paying only for services received. If costs turned out to be low, this would be an advantage.

(2) From the residents' standpoint the choice of specialists would be increased since, when it was determined that a specialist was needed, the resident could choose from the physicians throughout the entire area. (Such choice, of course, is subject to the approval of the staff physicians.)

(3) Availability of medical benefits while traveling.

DISADVANTAGES

(1) While there is a fixed fee from a medical services standpoint, there is not a fixed budget from an operating standpoint. In other words, there is an open end insofar as
medical expenses are concerned. Medical costs may be
considerably lower; they may run considerably higher. The
overall medical-hospital costs at one project, for example,
represented approximately 22 per cent of the total operating budget. Medical costs are an extremely important
budget item and if handled on an open-end basis could
present a serious liability.

(2) Medical services on the premises may be limited due to the
relatively small retainer which physicians are paid.

Contracting with a Clinic

In this third approach the clinic is paid a fixed fee per resident
per month to include all physicians' services, including the services
beyond the scope of the clinic, when such specialists are required.

ADVANTAGES

(1) It is the simplest and most direct method of achieving nearly
total medical care.

(2) It is economically the soundest since the medical costs are
assured for the length of the contract.

(3) Should costs run high, the clinic will give ample time to
make fee adjustments, changes in policy, and so on.

(4) Its success has been proven in practice.

(5) The scope of services available without an additional consultant's fee is greater, and therefore the advantages of
specialization can be realized more fully. If, for example,
a resident were examined by an internist who decided that
the advice of a gynecologist were necessary, the resident
would simply be referred to another specialist without additional cost to the project.

(6) On a fixed-fee basis the clinic is able to assume a risk of
unexpected medical costs which it can absorb more easily
than the residence, since the outlay of the clinic would be

only in services rendered or time expended whereas the financial outlay by the residence would be in cash, which could adversely affect its operating budget.

(7) Medical services generally not given can be offered. For example, ophthalmology, which may be an exclusion in the care agreement, can be covered up to the point of where it becomes economically impracticable.

DISADVANTAGES

(1) Limitation in the number of physicians available to a resident.

(2) Possible payments in excess of services offered. (There can be a clause in the contract allowing for negotiations upward or downward in price, of course.)

(3) Because the contract is with a clinic, physicians' services are limited to the area in which the clinic members practice.

Prior to Medicare only method 5.1c was acceptable; now, either method *b* or *c* is acceptable, subject to the cooperation of nonclinic physicians relative to Medicare billing problems.

5.2 Medical Center (Long-Term-Care Unit) Operation
5.20 Furniture

The operating costs of any long-term care unit are affected by the type of furniture used. It is possible, for example, to have fully automatic equipment, a single piece of equipment that allows a patient to adjust his bed, talk to the nurse, operate the television, and so on. Obviously, this is more expensive than a simple, manually operated bed with a conventional call system. The budget replacement cost is also more expensive. From the standpoint of labor costs, however, it is less expensive. All in all, the decision as to degree of refinement is a management decision based upon the extent of chronic care offered and the limitation of the budget.

5.21 Supplies

The amount of money spent upon supplies will vary with the scope and extent of care. A facility with a dispensary but without bed care will spend very little. Facilities giving bed care will spend greater amounts as the bed care approaches general hospital care.

5.22 Laundry and Cleaning and 5.23 Linen Replacement

The same considerations apply to these items as to items 2.4 and 2.5. The problem is, however, more complex. For instance, there is little chance in calculating the incident of incontinent patients.

If possible, even if a residence is laundering its own residence linen, the medical-unit linen should be contracted to avoid the danger of infection. (If a contract is impossible, the linen, of course, must be segregated from other linen and great care taken to avoid infection.)

5.3 Insurance

This item is concerned with residences which buy common commercial policies and are planning to provide medical care without approaching total care. There is a vast difference in coverage as well as cost; a discussion of commercial policies would be out of place in this work.

5.4 Malpractice Insurance

Irrespective of the diligence of management, it is essential to carry malpractice insurance. Surprisingly enough, it is relatively cheap insurance and, in most cases, will cost less than $1,000 per year.

5.5 Stop-loss Policy

With the ever-increasing number of residences for the elderly, certain insurance carriers have taken the opportunity of writing stop-loss policies which, in essence, are nothing more than inclusive group hospitalization policies (general hospital only, usually) with large deductibles. A typical example would be a policy for a small residence, covering hospital costs up to $100,000 and having a deductible of $30,000. Usually, such policies are quite reasonable since the carrier would be surprised if it ever had to pay any benefits whatsoever. Prior to Medicare it was an excellent idea to write the policy for the first year of operation or at least during the time the budget fund is accumulating; now it is no longer necessary. The value of such a policy would be limited to housing in which the ages of the residents averaged less than sixty-five.

5.8 Medical Payroll*

This, within ten years of operating experience, will become the largest single medical cost if an adequate long-term-care unit is provided. There are six basic categories of medical employment:

a. Nursing-department head.

b. Registered Nurse.

c. Licensed Vocational Nurse (or Licensed Practical Nurse).

d. Nurse's aide (or practical nurse).

e. Orderly.

f. Physical therapist.†

Categories *b* through *f* are self-explanatory.

Nursing-department Head

Some administrators favor a Licensed Vocational Nurse as department head because "RN's are frustrated MD's continually looking for ailments." This is a simple personnel problem and is, in our opinion, unjustified. Geriatrics nursing demands the most intensive nursing experience and continually necessitates on-the-spot decisions.

A resident stricken late at night demands immediate action. A nurse of less training than an RN may have to call an RN before she calls a physician. It is our strong recommendation to budget for twenty-four-hour RN coverage. (A registered nurse with a strong background in geriatrics nursing and a true sense of humanism will be most successful.) Any facility hoping to qualify for extended-care benefits under Medicare must have twenty-four-hour RN coverage, at least.

The basic staff will consist of three registered nurses (day, evening,

---

*Items 5.6 and 5.7 are unassigned.

†In a medical center of over fifty beds, a full-time physical therapist may be practicable. At one time, for example, a stroke victim was destined to lie in bed until he died. This is no longer true. Often it is possible to rehabilitate patients who but a decade ago were all but given up as hopeless.

night), one of which may be the department head. From this basic staff the personnel complement will expand according to the number of patients. The total nursing staff should equal between 2.0 and 4.5 hours of nursing care per patient-day, depending upon the medical needs of the specific group of patients receiving bed care.

In our projects we have instituted a training course to prepare nurses' aides for geriatrics work. In addition to typical duties, geriatrics patients require a greater amount of "tender and loving care" than any other patient group. Here it is most important to emphasize the continual necessity of purging the nursing department of the competent but hard-boiled. Geriatrics nursing is difficult at its best. It is not uncommon to see nurses leave a chronic-care hospital because of the hopelessness of terminal illness, the inveterate loneliness of chronic patients, and the despair of physical debilitation.

Using West Coast salaries in an area not subject to union jurisdiction, there is no personnel classification that has a greater variance in fringe benefits. Those, other than union standards, which must be investigated are as follows:

 a. Difference in pay scale among lesser-trained nurses.

 b. Difference in day, evening, and night pay.

 c. Holiday, vacation, and sick leave.

 d. Meal provisions.

 e. Uniform provisions.

 f. Split-shift provisions.

 g. Part-time or temporary provisions.

CATEGORY 6—REPLACEMENT RESERVES

During the estimated life of a building it is obvious, contrary to the Deacon's "one-hoss shay," that some parts will wear out before others and require replacement. It should also be observed that the style or fashion of some items such as plumbing fixtures or hardware may become quickly dated and must be renewed to retain a high tenancy rate.

From these two classes of reserves we may estimate the number of times during the economic life of the building that an object must be replaced. If we multiply the cost of these items (including installation) times the replacement period and subtract the salvage value, we will know within a reasonable degree of accuracy the funds we must set aside to meet these obligations. A curve then can be simply projected to indicate the amounts required at any particular period or year.

Under the first heading, "objects that wear out," are two types of items:

a. Those with moving parts, such as fans.

b. Those that oxidize or deteriorate, such as roofing or flashing.

Under the second heading, "style," are the following:

a. Items that can be changed with ease, such as hardware knobs or levers.

b. Items that may involve several trades, such as plumbing fixtures or elevator cabs.

A check-list of items follows, together with a salvage-value estimate, and a range of useful life:

Item	Salvage Value (%)	Useful Life (Yrs)	Comments
Waterproofing	—	?	Almost all masonry buildings require some waterproofing at some time.
Asphalt shingles	—	12-15	
Wood shingles	—	15-25	
Asbestos shingles	—	25-30	
Built-up roofing	—	10-30	Dependent on quality and plies.
Galvanized-iron flashing	—	15-20	
Caulking	—	10-30	Modern plastics will increase these estimates.
Interior marble	—	30	Usually, refinishing only, required.
Asphalt tile	—	10-15	
Vinyl tile	—	15-25	
Hardware	10	25	Heavy-duty hardware should last the building life, although design changes may be re-required.
Screens (insect)	—	15-25	Depends on material selected for both screens and frames.
Weather stripping	—	10-25	
Venetian blinds	—	10-20	
Kitchen sinks & fittings	5-10	25-30	
Lavatories & fittings	5-10	25-30	
Toilets & valves	5-10	25-30	
Tubs & fittings	5-10	25-30	
Washing machines	10-15	10-20	The rate of use of both washing machines and dryers varies widely. An analysis of mineral content might indicate that a filter would prove economical.
Hot-water system	—	20-30	
Heater-tank combination	—	5-15	

Item	Salvage Value (%)	Useful Life (Yrs)	Comments
Boilers	5	20-30	
Valves-pumps	5-10	20-30	
Compressors	10	15-25	
Fans	10	10-20	Usually motors only.
Electrical fixtures	—	20-25	
Elevator cabs & doors	—	20-30	
Hoists, cables & mechanical equipment	—	20-30	
Kitchen cabinets	—	20-30	
Refrigerators	5-10	10-12	
Ranges	5-10	10-12	

A final item that cannot be estimated because it extends into the unknown is the cost of alterations and additions that may be required by innovations or inventions. The depreciated tax-life of a fireproof structure is about fifty years. If we subtract these years from this year's date and consider the inventions in the intervening years, the magnitude and uncertainty of this part of the projection is evident.

This Category, Replacement Reserves, concludes the Statement of Operations, and the total of the listed items equals the Annual Operating Expense, as referenced in the following *Pro Forma* Statement of Operations (Appendix B).

Appendix A
PROJECT SUMMARY

Type	Rooms		Apartments			Residents		Entrance Fees		Monthly Income		
	Unit	Total	Single	Double	Total	Unit	Total	Unit	Total	Mo	Yr	Total
(and so on)												
Total												
Other Income												
Total												
95% Occup.												

Appendix B

PRO FORMA STATEMENT OF OPERATIONS

A. ESTIMATE OF ANNUAL OPERATING EXPENSE

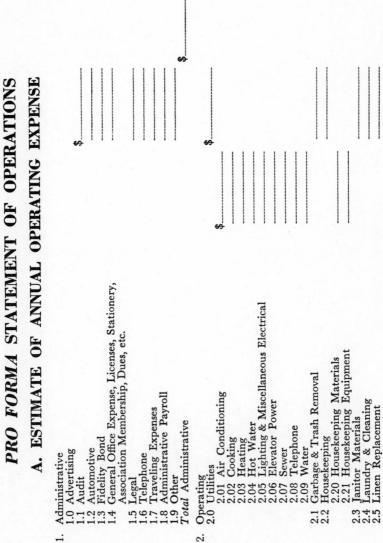

1. Administrative
   1.0 Advertising
   1.1 Audit
   1.2 Automotive
   1.3 Fidelity Bond
   1.4 General Office Expense, Licenses, Stationery, Association Membership, Dues, etc.
   1.5 Legal
   1.6 Telephone
   1.7 Traveling Expenses
   1.8 Administrative Payroll
   1.9 Other
   Total Administrative

2. Operating
   2.0 Utilities
      2.01 Air Conditioning
      2.02 Cooking
      2.03 Heating
      2.04 Hot Water
      2.05 Lighting & Miscellaneous Electrical
      2.06 Elevator Power
      2.07 Sewer
      2.08 Telephone
      2.09 Water
   2.1 Garbage & Trash Removal
   2.2 Housekeeping
      2.20 Housekeeping Materials
      2.21 Housekeeping Equipment
   2.3 Janitor Materials
   2.4 Laundry & Cleaning
   2.5 Linen Replacement

APPENDIX B (Continued)

2.6 Resident Transportation
2.7 Window Cleaning
2.8 Operating Payroll
2.9 Other

Total Operating $_____

3. Maintenance

3.0 Contract Services
  3.01 Elevators
  3.02 Exterminators
  3.03 Patrol Service
  3.04 Watchman Service
  3.05 Miscellaneous Appliances (Repairs)
3.1 Decorating
3.2 Furniture & Furnishings
  3.20 Carpets
  3.21 Draperies
  3.22 Furniture
3.3 Ground Materials & Equipment
3.4 Insurance
  3.41 Fire
  3.42 Furniture & Furnishings
  3.43 Liability
  3.44 Property
  3.45 Other
3.5 Repairs & General Maintenance
3.6 Vehicles
  3.60 Interest & Amortization
  3.61 Maintenance
  3.62 Repairs
  3.63 Rentals
3.7 Unassigned
3.8 Maintenance Payroll
3.9 Other

Total Maintenance $_____

APPENDIX B (Continued)

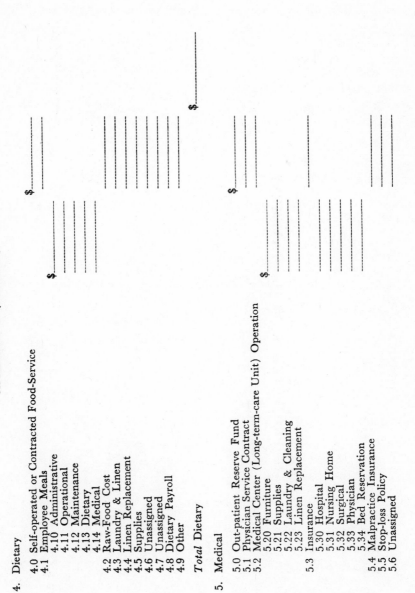

4. Dietary

    4.0 Self-operated or Contracted Food-Service $_____

    4.1 Employee Meals

       4.10 Administrative

       4.11 Operational

       4.12 Maintenance

       4.13 Dietary

       4.14 Medical

    4.2 Raw-Food Cost $_____

    4.3 Laundry & Linen

    4.4 Linen Replacement

    4.5 Supplies

    4.6 Unassigned

    4.7 Unassigned

    4.8 Dietary Payroll

    4.9 Other

Total Dietary $_____

5. Medical

    5.0 Out-patient Reserve Fund $_____

    5.1 Physician Service Contract

    5.2 Medical Center (Long-term-care Unit) Operation $_____

       5.20 Furniture

       5.21 Supplies

       5.22 Laundry & Cleaning

       5.23 Linen Replacement

    5.3 Insurance

       5.30 Hospital

       5.31 Nursing Home

       5.32 Surgical

       5.33 Physician

       5.34 Bed Reservation

    5.4 Malpractice Insurance

    5.5 Stop-loss Policy

    5.6 Unassigned

APPENDIX B (Continued)

B. PROJECTED ANNUAL STATEMENT

1. Income (from Project Summary) $ _____
2. Expense
       Operating expense (from A) $ _____
       Management fee _____
       Taxes
          Real estate _____
          Personal property _____
       Total expense $ _____
3. Cash Available for Debt Service
       Income (from B-1) $ _____
       Less expense (from B-2) _____
       Cash available for debt service $ _____
4. Debt Service
       Estimated development cost _____
       *Less entrance fees allocated to construction _____
       Amount of mortgage _____
          Total annual fixed charges $ _____
       Operating surplus (deficit) _____
5. Source of Funds to Extinguish
       Deficit
       †Interest on reserve fund $ _____
       Donations _____
       From reserve fund _____
          Total $ _____

5.7 Unassigned _____
5.8 Medical Payroll _____
5.9 Other _____
    Total Medical $ _____
6. Replacement Reserves _____
    Total Operating Expense $ _____

*Total entrance fees $_____

Less operating reserve for

  management and welfare $_____

Balance allocated to construction $_____ @ _____ % = $_____

†Interest on operating reserve

INDEX